T0328861

Many people believe that industrial relations have been transformed. For some, current developments are the result of new human resource management techniques which have overcome adversarial workplace traditions. For others, old attitudes remain, their expression stifled by vigorous competition in product and labour markets. *Willing slaves?* explores these competing claims. It shows that managers have come to question past approaches to employee relations. Nowadays they believe that 'winning workers' hearts and minds' is a crucial part of successful management. Equally, however, managers have not yet found ways to make their new ideas work well. Workers continue to place little trust in management, inefficient working practices persist, and attempts to build a 'new industrial relations' have fallen short of the mark. *Willing slaves?* concludes by arguing that the best way forward is for organisations to commit themselves to long term labour relations policies which enable workers to participate in management decision-making.

Cambridge Studies in Management 21

Willing slaves?

Cambridge Studies in Management

Formerly Management and Industrial Relations series

Editors
WILLIAM BROWN, *University of Cambridge*
ANTHONY HOPWOOD, *London School of Economics*
and PAUL WILLMAN, *London Business School*

The series focuses on the human and organisational aspects of management. It covers the areas of organisation theory and behaviour, strategy and business policy, the organisational and social aspects of accounting, personnel and human resource management, industrial relations and industrial sociology.

The series aims for high standards of scholarship and seeks to publish the best among original theoretical and empirical research; innovative contributions to advancing understanding in the area; books which synthesise and/or review the best of current research, and aim to make the work published in specialist journals more widely accessible; and texts for upper-level undergraduates, for graduates and for vocational courses such as MBA programmes. Edited collections may be accepted where they maintain a high and consistent standard and are on a coherent, clearly defined, and relevant theme.

The books are intended for an international audience among specialists in universities and business schools, undergraduate, graduate and MBA students, and also for a wider readership among business practitioners and trade unionists.

For a list of titles in this series, see end of book

Willing slaves?

British workers under human resource management

Andrew Scott

CAMBRIDGE
UNIVERSITY PRESS

CAMBRIDGE UNIVERSITY PRESS
Cambridge, New York, Melbourne, Madrid, Cape Town, Singapore,
São Paulo, Delhi, Dubai, Tokyo, Mexico City

Cambridge University Press
The Edinburgh Building, Cambridge CB2 8RU, UK

Published in the United States of America by
Cambridge University Press, New York

www.cambridge.org
Information on this title: www.cambridge.org/9780521467193

First published 1994

A catalogue record for this publication is available from the British Library

Library of Congress Cataloguing in Publication Data

Scott, Andrew.
Willing slaves? : British workers under human resource management
/ Andrew Scott.
    p.   cm. – (Cambridge studies in management: 21)
Includes bibliographical references.
ISBN 0–521–41257–9
1. Industrial relations—Great Britain—Case studies.
2. Industrial management—Great Britain—Employee participation–
–Case studies.   I. Title.   II. Series.
HD8391.S38   1994
331'.0941—dc20   93-23461   CIP

ISBN 978-0-521-41257-5 Hardback
ISBN 978-0-521-46719-3 Paperback

Contents

Tables

Acknowledgements

The debts I have incurred in researching and writing this book are too numerous and too great to be repaid. I owe an enormous debt of gratitude to the managers, union representatives, and workers in the workplaces that I visited. Their willingness to help me, their patience in answering what often must have seemed like naive and irrelevant questions, greatly increased my knowledge of workplace relations. I am indebted also to Nuffield College, where I completed my D.Phil, and the Advisory Conciliation and Arbitration Service (ACAS), where my D.Phil became this book. Both institutions provided generous support in helping me to take forward and refine my ideas. ACAS in particular allowed me the time and resources to complete this venture without constraining my personal interpretation of events. Throughout my research and writing the late Eric Batstone and subsequently Paul Edwards gave me thoughtful and constructive advice. Bill Hawes was an unfailing source of encouragement and good humour, and read my drafts more often than I had a right to expect. Veronica Maddison and Alan Felstead helped me to shape my ideas as the text neared completion. Finally, as ever, I owe my deepest debt to Hilary Pearce.

1   Co-operation at work?

Market pressures and the growth of 'realism'

The incompetent manager and the bloody-minded shop steward were for many years the stock-in-trade characters in 'tales of the shop floor'. Their disappearance from stories of more recent times may reflect a transformation in industrial relations. Many people believe that British workers are now working harder and more effectively than in the past. For some, these changes are evidence of a radically altered balance of economic power. For others, they are proof that managers and workers have arrived at a new level of understanding in their relations. What is certain is that changes in workplace behaviour have caused people to think afresh about the orthodoxy which permeated labour relations since the Second World War.

Many British industrial relations experts once placed their faith in collective bargaining to build constructive and co-operative relations on the shop floor. In Britain, the Donovan Commission (1968) concluded that collective bargaining could address and reconcile the inevitable differences of interest that arose between employers and their employees. It put forward the view that encouraging comprehensive workplace agreements could not only reduce adversarial behaviour but unite workers and managers in a common purpose. During the 1960s and 1970s such ideas were put into practice, and the proportion of British workers covered by collective bargaining increased. Formal systems of worker representation expanded as managers and a growing body of shop stewards engaged in local bargaining over a wider range of workplace issues (Parker 1975; Clegg 1979; Brown 1981; Daniel and Millward 1983). Public policy actively supported these developments. For example, the Employment Protection Act (1975) granted union members certain statutory rights to bargain with their employer, and at the same time the newly created Advisory Conciliation and Arbitration Service (ACAS) was charged with encouraging the reform and extension of collective bargaining throughout industry and commerce. The key to successful industrial relations was creating and sustaining an atmosphere in which constructive collective bargaining could take place.

Yet as collective bargaining spread more widely throughout the economy, so too did dissatisfaction with its results. Critics argued that its growing popularity in Britain throughout the 1960s and 1970s encouraged rather than eased industrial conflict. They contended that collective bargaining eroded management's 'right to manage' and that the problem of inefficient working practices and restrictive demarcations between jobs persisted. The result was not more orderly procedures for agreeing terms and conditions of work, but an increasingly inflexible set of arrangements whose adverse effect upon productivity weakened the ability of companies to compete in international markets (Metcalf 1989b). Today far fewer experts advocate the extension of collective bargaining as an essential ingredient of successful industrial relations. And there is clear evidence that an increasing number of employers are no longer prepared to follow the orthodoxy of the past. For example, many firms which previously bargained with trades unions over an extensive range of subjects now restrict joint discussions to a narrower set of issues. Some employers have made fundamental changes to their arrangements for union recognition, whilst others have increasingly preferred not to recognise trades unions at all in new workplaces (Millward *et al.* 1992; ACAS 1991a). The view that collective bargaining has failed to promote business success or to integrate the aspirations of employees with the goals of management seems to be widely held by experts and practitioners alike.

As the old orthodoxy has declined, what has taken its place? If many employers have turned away from the prescriptions of the past, have they found a successful alternative method of managing industrial relations? So far these questions remain open for debate, but whatever the course of change, it is likely to have been influenced by the widespread belief that the British economy reached a watershed in the 1980s. As changes in the nature of the international economy exposed enterprises to much greater competition, prominent managers identified the challenge facing modern organisations as the development of methods of decision-making which could successfully relate the size and shape of the workforce to their costs (Cadbury 1985). Others argued that workers had also increasingly come to accept that businesses which do not remain competitive must succumb to market forces. Recognising the ever-present threat which competition poses to the survival of organisations, it has sometimes been suggested that managers and workers nowadays share a similar view of the world. Their shared understandings, their common sense of 'realism' has, it is sometimes contended, forged a consensus upon how business and industrial relations must be conducted (Basset 1986).

It is not enough, however, to rest an account of change upon the assertion that 'realism' has pervaded British industrial relations. Whatever the truth of the matter, it requires further critical examination. How do managers and workers see and experience the 'reality' of commercial life? How profound is their shared understanding about the environment in which they work and make decisions? Within the existing literature it is possible to identify two distinctive accounts of the way in which managers and workers have responded to their more competitive circumstances.

The first possible explanation is of a traditional kind. It suggests that old attitudes have not been transformed but continue to exist, unspoken, pushed beneath the surface, their expression stifled by circumstance. Changes in the effort or application of workers have been the result of their being coerced into working harder, either directly by managers or indirectly by circumstance. They have responded, through want of an alternative, with grudging compliance rather than with enthusiasm. In this account, changes in workplace behaviour have been the consequence of an altered balance of power, and there has been very little change in underlying relationships between managers and workers: they continue to face each other in employment as adversaries, albeit less visibly so than in the past.

The second alternative and more novel view is that managers and workers have responded to new circumstances by building more constructive relations at work. In this more positive account of a 'new industrial relations' it has been suggested that the idea of a balance of power influencing decision-making in the workplace has become less relevant than it once was. Some managers claim to have found new and successful ways of fostering an identity of interests with their workers, and workers have responded by offering their best efforts to create a spirit of mutual co-operation.

The purpose of this book is to add to the debate upon how managers and workers have in practice responded to the challenge of more competitive times. Is the traditional or the new account a more accurate reflection of modern developments? Is there perhaps an element of truth in both of them? The remainder of this chapter elaborates the traditional account of change, and then examines claims for the apparent success of the 'new industrial relations'. Careful sifting of the existing evidence reveals that both strains of thought leave important questions unanswered, but they are nevertheless helpful in bringing to the fore interesting questions about the nature of current management thinking. These are identified and explored in the three case study chapters (chapters 3, 4 and 5) in which particular attention is given to the way in which present industrial relations differ from traditional expectations and patterns of behaviour. Each of the case studies is of a long established manufacturing workplace. The products each produce are not technically complex, and their production processes are not at the forefront of technology. To some people, these may seem surprising or unlikely places to look for changes in industrial relations. Yet new thinking and modern circumstances have had an undeniable impact in these factories. And although workplaces of this type are less common than in the past, they will probably continue to be with us for some time to come, making a variety of staple products for consumption in increasingly competitive international markets. It is here that one might expect the 'problems' of the old industrial relations to be most acute, where the process of transformation has been most complex, and where the innovations of the 'new industrial relations' have had to work hardest to overcome the engrained attitudes of the past. The final chapter of this book (chapter 6) draws together evidence of the success with which new kinds of management initiative have fostered improved co-operation. Can the introduction of these new techniques give one cause to hope that a longstanding British legacy of poor industrial relations has, within a decade, been transformed?

The traditional account: managers and workers as continuing adversaries

Management attitudes

According to some commentators managers have increasingly taken the view that it is their 'right' to insist that workers behave according to their instructions. This new way of thinking has been at the expense of an earlier desire to seek agreement with workers over changes and improvements in production. In an influential article, Purcell reported that many of the managers he met in the course of teaching industrial relations at a business school during the early 1980s appeared to have lost all interest in securing change through agreement (Purcell 1982). Evidence from certain sectors of British industry where it was once commonplace for managers to take decisions jointly with worker representatives lends support to this view. For example, studies of the British motor industry have revealed management's new determination to take decisions alone, discarding former processes for arriving at decisions jointly with employees (Willman and Winch 1985; Marsden 1985). In a further example from the coal industry, Richardson and Wood reported that new management initiatives to control costs and a new payments system were successful in disciplining coal miners' efforts. During interviews it emerged that managers clearly believed that they now had much more power to manage production and to meet commercial targets (1989, p.50). Reliable surveys of management attitudes which might provide broader evidence are few and far between. But, on the basis of a small postal survey, Mackay (1986) concluded that such uncompromising attitudes had spread to a majority of British managers. Driven by an awareness of greater market competition, the ascendency of 'realism' may therefore have encouraged managers to believe that their decisions no longer required workers' approval.

The attitudes of workers and their unions

Alongside accounts of managers' new-found assertiveness have been complementary accounts of workers' acquiesence. According to many commentators workers have not offered the resistance to more stringent standards of discipline that they might have done in the past, but instead have responded by working harder and supplying greater effort (Nichols 1986; Nolan 1988; Metcalf 1989b). Their compliance with more exacting management regulation may not, however, reflect an inherent new enthusiasm for work, but rather lack of any alternative. In this way of looking at things, workers' enhanced motivation has been derived not from factors within the workplace but from developments in the labour market. Concluding his analysis of factors contributing to the rapid rise in productivity experienced during the first half of the 1980s, Metcalf suggested,

The crucial factor in explaining the growth of labour productivity between 1980 and 1985 was the employment reduction experienced between 1980 and 1982.... Fear [of unemployment] must be what matters here'. (Metcalf 1989b p.19)

In similar vein, some have argued that workers' fear of unemployment has reduced their former readiness to take part in industrial action against employers. Their acquiescence in the exercise of management prerogative may have been one of the most important factors in enabling employers progressively to restrict the range of subjects included within joint discussions. Changes in the law may also have deterred workers from pressing their case against management. Nowadays the law offers less support for the extension of collective bargaining, and recent reforms have progressively restricted workers' ability to take industrial action in the course of disputes with employers. For example, changes in the law have rendered trades unions and their officials liable to damages for loss incurred by employers as a result of industrial action in a wide range of circumstances, and strikers' protection from selective dismissal has been removed. Taken together, these restrictions have added to the difficulties and personal risks involved in organising strike action. In so doing, their effect may have been to substantially undermine trades unions' ability to support their position in bargaining with effective sanctions (Brown and Wadhwani 1990; Nichols 1990).

Other factors may also have conspired to impair the ability of trades unions to sustain their position as serious negotiators with management. The decline of manufacturing industry, and in particular the disproportionate closure of large factories, has contributed to a substantial decline in trades union membership since 1979, with little prospect of an upturn in the foreseeable future (Metcalf 1989a; Stevens and Wareing 1990). Where managers have refashioned business organisations in order to make them more responsive to changes in product markets, traditional arrangements for collective bargaining may also have come under pressure. A trend to decentralise business decision-making and to bring about a more immediate relationship between producers and consumers may have caused the pattern of negotiations to become fragmented. It is possible that certain groups of workers who once bargained together may have found themselves in competition with one another, making it harder for trades unions to retain their traditional bargaining objectives. Some authors have suggested that these developments have been reflected in a profound loss of confidence on the part of union representatives. They have argued that shop stewards' concerns have narrowed to the extent that they are nowadays concerned almost entirely with local establishment issues to the exclusion of broader matters affecting other parts of the organisation or industry in which they work (Brown 1983). For Tailby and Whitson (1989) the course of recent change has been determined almost exclusively by management, with workers' representatives playing only a marginal role:

The unions have been unable to exert much influence on either the pace or the direction of change since the late 1970s, often accepting a managerial logic of change as a response to seemingly irresistible external competition ... the re-establishment of managerial prerogative and the downgrading of collective bargaining have in many cases undermined the status of shop stewards, and a new emphasis on the 'individualised' employment relationship has been carried over into work organisation and the choice of technologies. (Tailby and Whitson, 1989 p.18)

Taken together, workers' embrace of 'realism' and other related changes in the legal and business environment may have undermined both their willingness and their ability to oppose management initiatives which adversely affect their interests. For Terry (1989) workplace trades unionism faces nothing less than a 'crisis' (p194) of aims and identity, no longer able to put forward a distinctive and convincing case on behalf of workers. As managers have become more confident and assertive in pursuit of distinctive aims, it may be that workers and their trades unions have felt it increasingly impossible to alter the course of change.

An alliance of insiders?

Despite managers' new confidence and workers' reluctance to press their case, the distinctive feature of traditional accounts is that both parties continue to believe that employment is an adversarial relationship. For example, Kelly and Richardson (1989) have suggested that managers' inclination to improve productivity primarily by increasing wages rather than through initiatives to improve trust between workers and managers serves as proof of how little they have changed their view of the employment relation:

The fact that managers were prepared to pay for the new working arrangements in this way meant that they were in effect making an alliance with the surviving workers, the insiders. This reduced the likelihood of a build up in resentments because no group remaining in the organisation was a clear loser. (Kelly and Richardson 1990 p.144)

The essence of this attempt to account for recent history is that workers have accepted an extension of managers' prerogative in return for higher wages. According to this view, managers and workers have continued to understand their relations primarily as an exchange of money for effort or a 'wage–effort bargain'. It is inevitable that within such a perspective managers and workers must regard their interests as opposed:

As wages are costs to the firm, and the deprivations inherent in effort mean costs to the employee, the interests of management and wage-earners are diametrically opposed ... The dominant motives of workers cannot be explained unless one assumes that in fact they do compare potential earnings with required effort intensity. (Baldamus 1961 p.105–107)

Looking at things in this way suggests that during the early 1980s managers may have taken advantage of the increased bargaining power granted to them by rising unemployment, applying measures to 'increase the degree of effort which the employee is expected to surrender to the firm' (Baldamus 1961 p.47).

Within the traditional account, recent changes in industrial relations have been mapped according to the shifting contours of the wage–effort bargain. Here it must be admitted that empirical proof has been hard to come by. In practice, it has proved hard to measure changes in workers' effort. There is no single coherent definition of 'effort' that might be applied to workers across the broad spectrum of employment. And it is well known that existing measurement techniques such as work-study depend to a considerable degree upon subjective judgements (Rogers and Hammersley 1954; Guest 1990). But despite these difficulties, and in the absence of anything more comprehensive, work-study data collected by researchers over a period of several years from a large panel of manufacturing workplaces has pointed to a potentially interesting interpretation of recent history. By using this data to construct an index of labour utilisation, Bennet and Smith-Gavine have suggested that the level of effort supplied by workers in manufacturing industry rose dramatically during the early 1980s, reaching a peak during 1983 (Bennet and Smith-Gavine 1988). After 1983, as the immediate threat of unemployment waned, the trend of the index indicated that managers and workers may have reappraised their wage–effort bargain. The effort bargain, which had moved into a state of extreme 'disparity' during the early 1980s, moved closer to a state of 'parity' or equilibrium. Sharp rises in real wages took place because employers felt obliged to compensate workers for their greater efforts. The relative absence of overt industrial conflict in recent years can therefore be accounted for by employers having bought peaceful relations with workers (Kelly and Richardson 1989).

In brief, according to the traditional account, despite a general absence of visible industrial conflict, an adversarial conception of the employment relation has continued to permeate the thinking of all managers and workers. Although there have been considerable changes in the international economy, changes in the attitudes of parties to the employment relationship have reflected nothing more than a re-calculated wage–effort bargain. The shifts evident in the conduct of industrial relations in recent years have reflected calculations based upon narrow short term interests and have been the product of a limited adjustment to circumstance.

The alternative account: a 'new industrial relations'

There is another, more iconoclastic account of the way in which relationships in employment have developed. Some commentators have pointed towards the growth of a 'new industrial relations', whose aim has been to foster a more positive and less adversarial organisation culture. The terms used to describe the broad approaches used in these endeavours have varied. Of late, the management of 'human resources' has come into vogue at the expense of the management of 'personnel' and 'industrial relations'. In this book, new techniques which have emphasised that employment should be founded upon extensive mutual obligations and a sense of shared dedication towards a common goal are generally referred to as contributing towards a 'new industrial relations'. First illustrated by American scholars from the late 1970s onwards, this term encompasses the growing body of management beliefs and employment practices directed towards 'winning the hearts and minds' of employees in order to build a common commitment to organisational advancement (Walton 1985; Kochan *et al.*

1986; Capelli and McKersie 1987). These new management beliefs and policies are elaborated below.

New management attitudes

It may be that managers have developed new ways of managing industrial relations which are intrinsically more successful than earlier approaches. The stimulus for the development and application of these new techniques has been the intensification of international competition. Their distinctive character stems from an attempt to persuade workers to give their best efforts to the enterprise for which they labour. It is possible that the 'new industrial relations' has been the result of a happy coincidence of modern developments. Increased competition may have caused employers to develop new forms of decision-making which have proved not only more efficient but which have also made work more satisfying for workers. Furthermore, new forms of work organisation, often aided by new technology, may have ensured that deprivation is no longer inherent in effort. If these claims are true, then the idea of a wage–effort bargain is no longer relevant, and it is possible that harmonious and co-operative relations will become increasingly widespread in employment.

Evidence of changes in the attitudes of senior managers was provided in an interview survey organised by Edwards (1985a, 1985b). The survey was unusual in that it reported the views of senior production or works managers rather than personnel specialists. The results suggested that these managers, who have in the past often been associated with antipathy towards the personnel function, have now come to believe that employee relations policies are influential in contributing to business success. Edwards found that a substantial minority of works managers judged employee involvement and open management to be important features of effective personnel policies. He concluded,

The implication is that there is a widespread desire to go beyond reliance on traditional methods of collective bargaining so as to establish a more positive and less of a 'them and us', approach to industrial relations. (Edwards 1985a p.6)

Not only did the managers who were surveyed state their belief that success in business now depends upon the co-operation and integrated efforts of all employees, many of them also said that they measured their own success by the extent to which they convinced workers of their case for change:

To the extent that they had secured a change of attitude on the shop floor, the managers could feel that they had coped successfully. In doing so they used a policy based on co-operation . . . and not confrontation with the shop stewards. (Edwards 1985b p.8)

Further examples of a 're-orientation of management thinking' have been provided by Storey (1988 p.25; 1992). He has argued that during the 1980s managers became progressively more enthusiastic about new techniques which introduced change by fostering an atmosphere of consent and goodwill. An important feature of these new techniques was that they emanated not from personnel and industrial relations management but rather from a wider variety of business managers. It may be that an increased number of managers from all functions in business have come to believe that staff motivation and development has become a more important aspect of their work.

It may also be the case that managers have started to explain and justify to employees their reasoning for business decisions in a more systematic and convincing manner than hitherto. Survey evidence has suggested that some managers have put a belief in more open management into practice. They have claimed to consult workers or their representatives on a wider range of issues than in the past, and they may also have paid closer attention to maintaining effective means of communication and consultation (ACAS 1991, Scott 1991). Methods of communicating and consulting directly with employees, for example through team briefing and the use of quality circles, may also have sometimes augmented more traditional methods such as joint consultative committees which relied solely upon worker representatives, (ACAS 1991a; Millward et al. 1992). Qualitative evidence from case studies has suggested that initiatives to involve employees directly in the affairs of the company have sometimes been actively supported by union representatives, and according to both management and workers have led to an improvement in work relations (Marchington et al. 1992). Together these findings point to the potential development of a more 'open' management style in which 'adversarial relations' have at least in part given way to an approach in which all parties may have been more inclined to stress their common interests.

These developments in the management of industrial relations, perhaps brought about by personnel and production managers working more closely together, have produced new thinking about worker motivation and the efficient organisation of production. New approaches often seem to have required that employees perform a wider range of tasks whilst working in teams which have considerable autonomy. Kochan et al. (1986) have argued that the clear trend in job re-design in the USA has been to decentralise management authority and increase the degree of task-related problem-solving. Many British companies have also adopted similar working practices such as 'just-in-time production' and 'total quality management', requiring that workers be given greater authority to control and even stop production without the direct permission of management (Oliver and Wilkinson 1988). From a managers' point of view, Wickens

(1987) has argued that competitive standards of quality have their roots in an environment in which the views of workers are directly and continuously incorporated into new production methods. Wickens has stated that 'we regard it as part of everyone's job to strive to improve continuously' (p.72). Behind these developments there may be a new article of modern management faith emerging. Kochan has observed that managers in the USA who are implementing personnel policies to improve workers' commitment have increasingly come to believe that,

if workers can be motivated and given the opportunity to participate in the search for improved methods of job performance, and if this motivation can be sustained over time, job performance should improve. (Kochan *et al.* 1986 p.87)

The current attachment to this view is reflected in new management thinking about motivation techniques. In some workplaces, traditional types of incentive schemes have given way to 'pay-for-knowledge' systems:

Flexibility is designed into the new systems by having a small number of broad job classifications, few rules governing specific job assignments, less restrictions on work supervisors can perform, and more limited weight given to seniority in promotion and transfer decisions. In its most complete form this model replaces individual job assignments with team or group forms of work organisation and compensation. (Kochan *et al.* 1986 p.96)

Whatever their effectiveness, the development of these new approaches suggests that managers have been thinking afresh about their relationship with workers. They represent a move away from the belief that problems of motivation and questions of fairness can be settled by linking pay to fluctuations in effort. Instead, workers have been encouraged to develop further skills and use them wherever possible to promote efficient production. Situations in which there was once endless bargaining about rates, serving only continuously to remind parties of differences in their interests, may now be avoided. Arguments about relativities and the 'rate for the job', may have given way to an elaborate series of training steps and 'objective' appraisals of competence by management. Where such changes have taken place, they may point towards the development of a more sophisticated view of the employment relationship. For managers, those in their employ may no longer be considered as short term variable costs but long term investments whose effectiveness depends upon appropriate development (Marchington and Parker 1988). Where parties have become committed to the development of their relationship in the longer term, it may now have become increasingly possible for managers to offer guarantees of job security in return for workers providing corresponding guarantees of flexibility, thereby effecting a substantial improvement in trust.

Taken together, these developments suggest that management may have been reappraising its relationship with workers in quite fundamental ways. It may be that some managers have become dissatisfied with employment based upon an adversarial exchange of money for effort, and have instead sought to reconstruct their relationships along more sophisticated lines. The shifting emphasis in the direction of communication with individual employees, closer relations between supervisors and workers and the establishment of performance appraisal may have had profound implications for organisation culture. Furthermore, where standards of performance and discipline have been set in new and different ways, the scope for workers legitimately to challenge these processes may also have been altered. For example, Guest (1989a, 1989b) has argued that the philosophical underpinning of the 'new industrial relations' presumes that there should be no conflict between the interests of employees and the management of an organisation. In this sense, it advances a vision of the ideal organisation which amounts to a form of sophisticated unitarism. Its policy prescriptions may have eschewed the overtly brutal suppression of dissent associated with the unitarism of old (Fox 1974), but nevertheless they have advocated practices which might have inhibited employees' belief that their interests were separate and distinct from those of management. Within the perspective of a more sophisticated modern unitarism, managers may have been engaged in refashioning employee relations in ways that have encouraged workers to relate to the organisation as individuals, rather than primarily as members of a distinctive interest group. In such circumstances, the scope for trades unions to operate may have been reduced. What role is left for them in the 'new industrial relations'?

The future role of trades unions

The development of the 'new industrial relations' has raised a question-mark over the modern role of trades unions. In Britain, recent survey evidence has revealed that the range of issues included within collective bargaining has declined. Some employers have simplified their dealings with trades unions by streamlining recognition arrangements and, in a small but growing number of instances in which unions have been derecognised, it may be that an increasing number of employers have come to believe that it is possible to operate without any unions at all (Millward *et al.* 1992). Fewer employers establishing new plants have chosen to recognise trades unions, and it seems clear that many employers no longer regard them as an essential ingredient of successful industrial relations. Where managements were able to limit the scope of union activity during the recession of the early 1980s, it may be that the subsequent introduction of new policies improved industrial relations to such a degree that employees no longer felt that trades union membership could bring further benefit. There may be several reasons for this.

Under collective bargaining the function of workplace rules was partly to restrict the discretionary power of management. According to some authors this inevitably resulted in labour relations policies in which collective interests dominated at the expense of allowing individual talents to flourish. Exponents of the 'new industrial relations' have suggested that an informal and flexible approach to rule-making can displace traditional bureaucratic approaches. More capable of recognising and rewarding differences in individual talent, these approaches may have led to the development of more fulfilling work relationships. Survey evidence from the USA has suggested that in workplaces where 'new industrial relations' policies have been implemented, there is a reduced probability of union recognition (Evansohn 1989). The hallmark of the 'new industrial relations' may therefore be that

[it] rejects or ignores the need to provide independent structures and procedures for articulating and accommodating these diverse interests. Instead informal participation processes and enhanced planning and communications are expected to serve as substitutes for the adversarial procedures of collective bargaining, contractual rules and grievance arbitration. (Kochan *et al.* 1986 p.208)

If management's disposition towards rule-making has changed in this direction, it need not necessarily have manifested itself in overt antipathy towards established workplace unionism. Indeed it is striking that in British workplaces which have well developed union recognition arrangements, these seem to have been left virtually intact over the past decade (Millward *et al.* 1992). Yet even where managements may not have deliberately tried to reduce the institutional influence of unions in recent years, other changes in the direction of more open management may have rendered trades unions less relevant to the conduct of employee relations (Marchington and Parker 1990 p.228). For example, improvements in the training and selection of supervisors may have made disputes based upon arbitrary decisions less likely (Wickens 1987). More generally, decentralisation of management decision-making may have provided people with an opportunity to understand management objectives in a way not possible hitherto. For example, one senior influential manager has written that such developments in organisation structures offer employees 'the prospect of more control over their working lives' (Cadbury 1985 p.21). In these circumstances, the role of trades unions may have become restricted to securing fairness where management makes decisions which 'fail to consider fully the interests of the company'. Their overriding objective may have become 'working for the long-term success of the enterprise and its employees' (Wickens 1988 pp.24–29). It may be that where managements have implemented the prescriptions of the 'new industrial relations', trades unions have found it increasingly difficult to pursue a distinctive and influential role.

Unanswered questions

Whatever path British employers have followed, whether it be to further an adversarial tradition or to develop a more sophisticated view of their relations with workers, our present understanding of each of these options raises a good many further questions.

The traditional account

If the traditional account of change is the most viable explanation of recent history, if an 'alliance of insiders' has really formed during the past few years, then it is necessary to explain how the alliance came about, and how it works in practice on the shop floor. The view that workers have agreed to more extensive management prerogatives in return for increases in real wages is too simple an explanation. For example, within the 'alliance', how far has management been able to achieve its aims? Have extensions of management prerogatives been rendered sufficiently acceptable to workers simply on account of higher wages? Answers to these questions must in turn lead one to consider why it is that workers might have agreed to work harder, accept tougher discipline or closer supervision, sometimes but not always in return for higher wages or the promise of a job for the following month.

The traditional account of change suggests that management's efforts to persuade workers of its case, through collective bargaining and by other means of involvement, have become a less important ingredient in ensuring successful industrial relations. One possible explanation for this is that employers may have relied increasingly upon a coincidence between product and labour market pressures, and workers' natural reticence openly to dispute management decisions. Armstrong et al. (1981) have argued, on the basis of detailed shop floor observation and interviews, that the language and ideas which contribute to social understandings about employment by and large favour the interests of management. Workers lack a coherent ideology of their own, and generally subscribe to moral values which have been derived from management ideology. They have therefore always been inclined to accept that managers have the right to determine which tasks they should perform, and to specify who should perform them. This has traditionally put them at a disadvantage in disputing management decisions and has provided scope for management to manipulate the wage–effort bargain in its own favour:

> The legitimising principles available to managers can be used to justify their rule-making in very general terms ... the principles available to workers, on the other hand, consist of isolated and specific rejection of managerial ideology and have greater limitation on what can be legitimised. (Armstrong *et al.* 1981 p.44)

In recent years management may have been able to exploit the prospect of a declining market share to an unprecedented degree. For example, when an employer has asserted that certain changes are necessary in order to keep up with the pressures imposed by competition or in order to prevent economic collapse and the threat of unemployment, workers may often have felt they have had little choice but to accept (Armstrong *et al.* 1981, Terry 1989). Taken together, these factors may have intensified the inherent difficulties which workers have always encountered in their attempts to fashion a legitimate case against management demands. Workers' natural disposition to accept that management arguments have superior moral authority may have been considerably reinforced and it may be that the modern wage–effort bargain has become still more elastic, capable of being stretched well beyond the limits to which it was subject in the past.

Yet although workers might have been prepared to put up with a worsening wage–effort bargain for a while, giving their all 'for the duration', is it likely that this state of affairs has persisted in the longer term? If firms have adopted a less 'lenient' approach in recent years, and have attempted to tighten discipline on the shop floor, it becomes important to consider what long term effect this might have had upon existing patterns of co-operation. The premise of the traditional explanation is that managements have placed less reliance upon joint decision-making and have increasingly made use of management fiat. But even in modern times the extent to which workers have accepted management values must at some point have found its limit, and it is therefore probable that employers have been able to manipulate the wage–effort bargain only within certain bounds. The effectiveness of management appeals to the situation in the product market may have waned as workers' sustained exertion has become wearisome and painful. Where employers have continuously insisted upon higher standards of effort over and above workers' judgements about what is 'reasonable', workers may not have offered outright opposition, but it is likely that they will have come to resent management's behaviour. Such resentments may have diminished their willingness to obey management instructions with vigour or enthusiasm:

> the implication of employees giving full consent is that they 'authorise' management

to govern them, thereby giving a special significance to the term 'authority'. Management can govern without this authority by employing coercion, but it faces at best passive indifference and at worst militant hostility. (Fox 1985 p.67)

If morale has declined it is likely to have had adverse consequences for the effort that workers put into their jobs. In the words of Phelps-Brown, 'to lose heart', after all, is almost synonymous for 'to do less' (Phelps-Brown 1949 p.49). He continued,

A job cannot be regarded only as so much work to be done for so much money, but must be seen and handled as a social situation in which there are many relations between the worker, his mates, his supervisors, his home and his pay. Influences other than the wage-incentive seem likely to be not merely propitious as establishing the sort of climate in which the wage-incentive can take hold, but themselves as strong as, or sometimes even stronger than the wage. (Phelps-Brown 1949 p.52)

In this view, where management attitudes have undervalued the benefits of high morale, there will have been a cost in terms of lost effort:

As a normal part of the relations of production, and not just to prevent antagonistic behaviour, those possessing formal authority enter into complex exchanges with those below them, and since the latter are not really powerless, these transactions are not one sided affairs, even if they are not evenly balanced. (Harris 1987 p.206)

In certain circumstances, 'tightening up' the wage–effort bargain might have eroded co-operation to the disadvantage of both managers and workers. Gouldner's (1955) classic account of mis-managing change provides an apt illustration of this point. Low wages and low productivity formed the basis of stable working relations between managers and supervisors at a rural mine. But the onset of recession and the appointment of new management led to a tightening of discipline, the development of a claim for better wages, and ultimately a bitter industrial dispute. After the dispute both productivity and wages improved, but the relations between managers and workers were difficult and unpleasant. The exchange of favours and acts of co-operation, once the hallmark of their relations, no longer took place. Productivity rose but the workers were no longer prepared to provide the extra effort necessary to meet orders in exceptional or unforeseen circumstances, effecting a reduction in flexibility. Clearly, although a new wage–effort bargain came about, the benefits of co-operation were not fully realised. The importance of 'goodwill' between workers and managers makes the suggestion that firms have responded to market competition by eliminating restrictive working practices a more complicated proposition than it at first sight seems. Where managements have neglected to convince employees in a positive way that they should support management goals, the effect of their behaviour upon workers' morale may have affected the rate at which workers have exerted themselves. Management may well have tried to tighten up on discipline and effort, but what has been the outcome?

In brief, employers ploughing a traditional furrow may have found that in practice their attempts to develop a more assertive style of management have been less successful than they hoped. It is interesting to examine whether or not they have preferred to press the advantages conferred upon them by the labour market in order to drive home the tightest possible wage–effort bargain. In the long term, the implication might be that either the 'alliance of insiders' will prove unworkable and give way to a more participative management approach, or that shop floor co-operation will become progressively more limited. In any event, it is important to explore what has happened to management authority and workers' morale on the shop floor.

The 'new industrial relations'

It is likely that the ideas behind the 'new industrial relations' have in part been influenced by managers' disappointments in the past. New approaches may have recognised that traditional views of employment as simply a collective wage-effort bargain have been insufficient to inspire high levels of morale or generate enthusiasm for work. Furthermore, it may be that not only did many managers find it difficult to make the old model work, but also that many now believe its aims have proved too limited for successful industrial relations in a modern business. Fox, once an advocate of collective bargaining, later expressed clear views about its limitations in this respect:

Collective bargaining can promote compliance by virtue of being a process through which employees secure, indirectly through representatives, a voice in the making of decisions important to them. Such a process ... can strengthen the legitimacy of rules in the eyes of the governed and thus increase the chances of their being accepted and obeyed ... There was no reason to suppose, however, that collective bargaining would generate within the individual employee the positive moral involvement in his job that management might be seeking. The fact that someone is participating on his behalf in other mens' decision-making does nothing to enrich the importance and quality of the decision he is currently called upon to make in his own job. (Fox 1985 p.112)

One might be forgiven for believing that many of the 'new industrial relations' prescriptions for reform have been tried before. For example, it has long been held that effective organisation depends upon management providing respected leadership. Similarly, many managers have long been aware of the benefits of 'putting workers in the picture'. And throughout the post-war period numerous experiments with job re-design have allegedly allowed workers to develop more fulfilling and co-operative relationships on account of the way their work is organised. All these longstanding ideas find a close parallel in the prescriptions for the 'new industrial relations' or 'human resource management'. But what is perhaps distinctive about current developments is the suggestion that management has combined these ideas and ascribed them a new importance in order to make an appeal to workers as individuals. Together these measures constitute an attempt to either integrate or incorporate workers as individuals within broader decision-making processes.

According to some commentators, this kind of appeal to individualism has come at a propitious time. Unprecedented prosperity may have brought about a profound change in the way workers comprehend the workings of society and their position within it. Nowadays their traditional views about work relations involving a profound and unbridgeable gap between 'us and them' may have been displaced by a faith in the diffusion of meritocratic values both throughout society as a whole and within their own workplace (Phelps-Brown 1990). Workers consequently may no longer tend to see their interests as distinct from, and opposed to, those of management but instead may share a belief that able individuals will rise within organisations and receive their just rewards. It may be that managements which have appealed to workers as individuals have struck a chord which is the basis for high morale and co-operative working.

Perhaps some caution is in order. Have workers really embraced the same values as managers to the point of complete convergence? Has all talk of interests been subsumed by the creation of meritocracy? It is difficult to know what to make of these possibilities. Whilst Phelps-Brown's views seem intuitively plausible, evidence from SCPR's British Social Attitudes Surveys presents a rather more traditional picture. Rather than suggesting that British workers have re-evaluated their position vis-à-vis their employer, it appears that most employees have continued to believe that their interests differ from those of management, and that trades unions continue to have a valuable role in the workplace (Brook et al. 1992). It is not possible to do more than mention these possibilities in passing here; they are part of a broader debate about the changing nature of modern liberal democratic societies. But they do suggest that it is important to explore the distinction between idealism and practice in the introduction of new ideas and practices on the shop floor.

Where the 'new industrial relations' has been put into practice, it is necessary to discover more about the precise nature of its appeal to managers and employees. For example, some commentators have suggested that rhetoric about the benefits which the 'new industrial relations' can bring for workers has tended to outstrip reality (Wells 1988; Guest

1990; Kelly and Kelly 1991). Whatever the truth of the matter, this possibility makes it important to examine the practical means by which managers' and workers' interests are supposedly reconciled. This inevitably must lead one to consider, for example, the nature and extent of shop floor workers' freedom to take decisions in setting production and quality standards. Equally it is important to recognise that the achievement of modern ideals may be tempered by workplace traditions. It is probable that the strength of 'them and us' feelings are not simply a reflection of what is happening in society as a whole, but also a reflection of workers' and managers' personal experience of life in a particular workplace. It therefore becomes important to ask whether organisations can escape from their past and eradicate longstanding traditions of wage–effort bargaining in favour of common commitment to a common purpose.

Some accounts of the 'new industrial relations' have drawn attention to improvements in the quality of workers' jobs. For example, Dawson and Webb (1989) visited an electronics plant where production had been organised on a 'just in time' basis and in which workers had been made responsible for quality control. From their account it appeared that workers experienced considerable autonomy and discretion in their work. Yet in the past other experiments in autonomous working have been judged less successful in their long term consequences. Beyond the rhetoric of managers' claims to be improving the quality of working life, it has sometimes been suggested that companies have often introduced autonomous groups in order to reduce staff requirements, with broader 'quality of working life' goals coming a very poor second (Kelly 1982). A recent account of working practices at a Japanese-owned car assembly plant in the UK has suggested that contemporary developments in working practices still have limited aims (Garrahan and Stewart 1989). Flexibility amounted to little more than learning a number of relatively simple jobs; teamworking meant doing them without question, often in addition to one's own job, when it was necessary to cover for sick or absent colleagues. Whether in the 'new industrial relations' attempts to reform job design have been more broadly based, providing workers with greater intrinsic satisfaction is, therefore, an important issue.

Closely related to these matters are further issues about the targets which workers are required to meet. In some reported examples of the 'new industrial relations' it appears that management has insisted that workers perform to high standards. For example, at the electronics plant studied by Trevor, employees were told in no uncertain terms during their induction course that very high levels of attendance were required of them and that regular absence, for whatever reason, would not be tolerated. At the car plant visited by Garrahan and Stewart, new production methods placed workers under high levels of continuous stress. Even though they believed that their jobs were secure and their prospects good, these traditional sources of anxiety were replaced by new ones based upon close monitoring of individual performance. Whether new approaches to job design have achieved success through fostering commitment, or have resulted in more stressful, tightly controlled work routines is therefore another issue worthy of further exploration.

Further questions arise about broader issues of worker representation and management decision-making. Once again, although existing empirical studies have been able to shed some light upon the various mechanisms which are supposed to integrate the interests of management and workers, the overall picture is by no means clear. In some workplaces, trades unions may have played a less important role, as employers have found other means of consulting and communicating with employees. Furthermore Marchington (1990) has suggested that some trades unions have willingly co-operated in developing direct communications between managers and workers, in ways which have been at the probable long term expense of collective bargaining. But can new systems of individual involvement actually lead to joint decisions? Trevor and White (1983) have suggested that British workers found the managers in a Japanese-owned plant more approachable than their traditional British counterparts. It may be that policies which have induced a climate of positive informal relations between managers and workers have enabled workers to approach managers directly with their problems without need of bureaucratic union apparatus. At the same time, however, workers may not always have felt able to place such faith in their individual relations with managers. For example, labour turnover at the electronics plant studied by Trevor, whilst below the industry average, still occurred at a rate of 15 percent. In the absence of any other explanation, this fact might be construed as evidence that in practice workers did not find it easy to present personal issues to their managers. No matter how good their personal relations were, these managers were after all, the very same people that were exhorting them to reach the highest possible production standards. In situations where there is little or no developed means of formal worker representation it is not yet clear whether policies which purport to encourage 'direct involvement' have allowed workers to make effective representation of their views. In the absence of further evidence, might it not equally be that the pressures placed upon workers to conform to management plans have been increased?

On the basis of this evidence, it is not yet clear that new 'co-operative' styles of management have secured workers' agreement to change. Although Trevor argued that workers were kept well informed of the deliberations of the Works' Council, and that they were provided with opportunities to subject management decisions to continual scrutiny and criticism, his case study did not yield examples of this process in action. Other accounts have been less positive. Dawson and Webb cited the views of managers who believed that change had been easier to introduce because they did not have to negotiate but merely consult with workers. They also suggested that the workers felt that changes in working methods had been imposed upon them. At the car plant visited by Garrahan and Stewart, management was portrayed as having successfully marginalised the trades union whilst it enjoyed virtually unlimited prerogative. It appears that rather than having persuaded workers of its case, management policies had served to restrict opportunities for workers to express feelings of dissent. Clearly, therefore, until more is understood about the way in which new techniques have elicited workers' co-operation in practice on the shop floor, it may be premature to suggest that managers and workers in the 'new industrial relations' have come to enjoy harmony and unanimity.

If the 'new industrial relations' has not effectively 'won the hearts and minds of workers', if these new techniques have failed to secure a high level of social integration within the workplace, is it possible that practices associated with the 'old' industrial relations have started to re-emerge on the shop floor? Already there is some evidence of this. For example, Lupton's (1963) description of working practices at an electrical engineering factory outlined at some length a collection of 'fiddles'. These were the deliberate disobedience of management rules by workers in the production process in order to make work easier or more satisfying. Lupton suggested that '"the fiddle" was a quite stable adjustment of the discrepant goals and interests of management and workers' (1963 p.197). Similarly, in the modern electronics factory studied by Dawson and Webb, it appeared that workers did not operate 'just-in-time' practices as they were supposed to, but instead built up buffer stocks between steps in the production process. They did this in order to avoid the stresses of having to solve the problem of why they ran out of parts in the first place: evidence perhaps, that even in the 'new industrial relations' workers have found it both desirable and possible to subvert management rules.

Variations in the practice of the 'new industrial relations' are likely to prove as interesting as the broad shape of the model itself. For example, it may be that in practice the new procedures have appeared to work because management was prepared to settle for something less than workers' complete commitment to the exercise. Sewell and Wilkinson have related the instance of a textile factory in which despite the introduction quality circles, managers and supervisors tacitly supported workers' falsification of production and quality statistics (1992 p.283). In Dawson and Webb's account, it was a manager who drew attention to workers' fiddles. He justified them by suggesting that 'it allows them [workers] to continue production when problems arise' (Dawson and Webb 1989 p.235), indicating that management in some circumstances may still be prepared to tolerate certain kinds of deviations from rules where they help to stabilise work relations.

Equally, however, management leniency over these matters may vary between workplaces. Some have argued that the introduction of 'just-in-time' and 'total quality management' techniques have granted managers the potential to exercise an unprecedented degree of control over work. Sewell and Wilkinson (1992) have illustrated their point with evidence from visits to an electronics plant where the production system embodied sophisticated electronic monitoring of work. Workers who produced sub-standard output were quickly detected by management. Similarly, they have drawn attention to the management practice in modern car factories of encouraging workers to engage in 'peer surveillance'. In these instances, one gains the impression that modern techniques for organising production have been accompanied by precious little management leniency. Yet although these studies underline the potential impact of management policies, they raise further and perhaps more important questions about their practical impact. What happens if and when management becomes dissatisfied with workers' performance? How does it tackle situations in which standards of performance slip? What are the consequences of 'tightening up' in a 'new industrial relations' workplace?

It is testimony to the extensive changes that have taken place in manufacturing industry in recent years that so many recent studies of the 'new industrial relations' have been located in relatively new workplaces. Others have examined the introduction of new policies in workplaces which seem to have been well placed to introduce change. For example, at the electronics plant visited by Cressey et al. (1985), managers had prided themselves for many years on a policy of open management, extensive consultation, single status, and high pay. This was a circumstance in which 'new industrial relations' policies were introduced into a factory in which it seems unlikely that there had ever been a visible tradition of effort bargaining. In other situations, however, the introduction of change and the benefits of 'new industrial relations' for management may not have been realised so easily; features of the old industrial relations may have altered the nature of new initiatives. For example, Lever-Tracey (1990) examined the introduction of quality improvement groups on a traditional Australian assembly line. The groups were set up by management to promote co-operation in essentially small ways beneficial to both management and workers. They suggested many worthwhile but relatively minor improvements in costs, quality production and plant safety, but at the same time they did not result in the elimination of traditional working practices (Lever-Tracey 1990 p.191). Whatever the potential of new techniques to strengthen management's control of work it is also possible that they have granted certain workers, in 'strategic' positions within the production process, new powers over management. For these reasons, workers may have been able to limit the demands which management can make of them, just as workers did in the automobile plants studied by Sayles (1958) over thirty years ago. Whether workers have combined to shape their terms and conditions of work may have depended upon their previous experiences of the way in which management behaved towards them. Away from 'greenfield' sites, transforming old industrial relations into 'new industrial relations' may not have been straightforward. Established patterns of behaviour may have constituted traditions that in themselves have exerted a powerful influence over attitudes towards change in mature industrial workplaces.

The ambition of the 'new industrial relations' to achieve a powerful synthesis of management and worker interests suggests that its successful implementation may require a good deal of commitment, foresight and planning on the part of management. In some Japanese-owned workplaces in the UK this may have been achieved to an impressive degree. For example, there can be little doubt that management at the Japanese-owned electronics plant visited by Trevor (1988) gave industrial relations a high priority. Managers firmly believed that there was an important link between high quality, highly adaptable production facilities and a committed flexible workforce. Where such commitment is present, the 'new industrial relations' may have brought good results. For example, the distinctive personnel policies at another Japanese-owned factory studied by Trevor and White (1982) appeared to go some way towards convincing employees that management took account of their interests. In an attitude survey, these workers expressed overwhelmingly favourable opinions of management, believing that it valued their efforts, and they judged their plant to be a better place to work than other local factories.

The question which follows inevitably is: can British companies introduce these changes successfully? In this respect, the historical evidence is less encouraging. Whatever the intrinsic limitations of collective bargaining as a means of employee involvement, its 'failure' was perhaps at least partly caused by the way in which managers attempted to put it into practice. The difficulties encountered in making the pluralist model work were perhaps due in no small part to lack of strategic thinking on management's part. Often new procedures were introduced without taking account of the ways in which they related to other functions of the business

(Blackler and Brown 1980). Furthermore, advocates of reform failed to convince workers and their representatives of the benefits of change. As a consequence, shop stewards' encounters with management in the course of collective bargaining did not serve to change their attitudes or values and 'rather than reformist measures changing the stewards, stewards changed the reformist measures' (Batstone 1988 p.224). Collective bargaining failed to bring about improved co-operation partly because the manner in which it was conducted by management limited the trust which bargaining parties were able to place in one another; the reform measures which were supposed to build involvement instead became used for the purposes of expressing dissent (Purcell 1981 pp.242–245).

Realising the ambitions of the 'new industrial relations', and achieving the powerful synthesis of interests between management and workers which it claims is possible, presents a challenge of equal or even greater complexity than the earlier reforms of industrial relations based upon collective bargaining. But if the successful implementation of the 'new industrial relations' has required a good deal of detailed forward planning on the part of management, can co-operative approaches to labour relations thrive in organisation cultures which contain a substantial element of 'muddling through'? Similarly where organisations have introduced change on an incremental basis, where attachments to old ideas exist alongside new ones, what progress can the 'new industrial relations' have made?

Conclusions

Growing awareness of world competition may have profoundly affected the way in which managers and workers have interpreted developments within organisations. Many accounts of change have been founded upon the idea that the imperative of economic reorganisation has equipped managers with a new sense of purpose. Either managers have capitalised upon the weakness of organised labour to make more stringent demands upon workers, or they have taken opportunities to fashion genuinely more co-operative labour relations.

Beneath the generality of these accounts, however, it may be taking too much for granted to tie explanations of change so closely to the influence of external factors. Within organisations, individuals may often have had some latitude to shape their relations in accordance with narrower priorities. If 'realism' is to have any useful meaning, one must explain how it has been created and sustained by managers and workers on the shop floor. Exploring developments in industrial relations inevitably raises questions about the ways in which past beliefs have co-existed or have been displaced by newer ideas. The belief that workers and managers have come to pursue more closely-related goals is now commonplace, but the extent of their rapprochement, and how it has been achieved, has remained an open question. Similarly it is interesting to consider whether managers, apparently free from the overt opposition of organised labour, have approached the management of labour relations with a coherence and professionalism not possible hitherto. Has economic reorganisation altered workers' traditional conception of their interests being distinct from those of management?

The following chapters look for further insights into these matters. Chapter 2 describes and explains the research methods used to conduct the three case studies which are the core of this book. Chapters 3, 4, and 5 present detailed accounts of each case, illustrating the extent to which new attitudes have developed and affected the behaviour of managers and workers on the shop floor. Chapter 6 compares and contrasts the three case studies with other empirical evidence, and advances some general thoughts on how shop floor relations are changing under modern competitive pressures.

2   The shop floor revisited

Introduction

It is impossible to capture a complete account of relations between managers and workers from the details of employment contracts or formal collective agreements: these relations often depend upon unwritten expectations or obligations. Illuminating these expectations, and examining the extent to which they receive practical expression and are reconciled, is the purpose of this book.

In many respects, the debate over the ways in which industrial relations is changing has never been so well informed. Evidence from large scale interview surveys, notably the ED/ESRC/PSI/ACAS Workplace Industrial Relations Surveys has enabled scholars and commentators to make deductions from extensive data of high quality. Yet the type of information which can be collected in large scale surveys is not best suited to our present purpose. For example, Millward *et al.* (1992) have charted a decline in the coverage and scope of collective bargaining, and suggested that traditional approaches to industrial relations are on the wane. But large scale surveys which rely upon highly structured questionnaires are an insensitive instrument with which to uncover and explore the new ideas which may be taking the place of past orthodoxy. Such enquiries depend upon systematically identifying particular kinds of institutions and practices, at a time when they may not have found their own distinctive means of expression. Millward *et al.* (1992, ch. 10) have gone some way to endorsing this point in explanation of why they can find so little trace of a new system of industrial relations to fill the gap brought about by change. Arguably this difficulty is partly a reflection of cross-sectional survey designs, and can be overcome to some extent by further proposed investigation of data collected from a panel of respondents (Millward and Daniel 1993). But Morris and Wood have gone further and argued that any method of investigation which relies upon highly structured interviews must inevitably result in a picture of management activity which is 'overformalised and rigid' (1991 p.265). They preferred to study change by means of less structured 'depth interviews' with managers, from which they concluded that a continuing formal commitment to collective bargaining can too easily hide the extent to which new ideas have taken shape in the past few years:

behind the facade of institutional stability, we found evidence that managers were changing or had changed the way institutions functioned, often in subtle ways. (Morris and Wood 1991 p.278)

Yet if in-depth interviews allowed managers to expand upon their ideas with greater freedom, Morris and Wood also openly acknowledged that their own approach had its limitations; for instance, they recognised that talking to managers alone might have produced an exaggerated account of the extent to which new thinking had been put into practice (p.278). Others (see, for example, Marchington and Parker 1990; Marchington *et al.* 1992) have attempted to overcome this problem by reviewing a broader range of evidence collected over an extended period of time. Such accounts, written up in the form of case studies, have drawn not only upon interviews with managers and employees but also upon the evidence of written management documents, and the minutes of management–union meetings. Research of this nature offers a better opportunity to learn about peoples' feelings towards industrial change, but it also furnishes an incomplete account of the social processes being enacted on the shop floor. Understanding how and why change has taken place requires some evidence of the ways in which new attitudes have been associated with changes in behaviour. A more comprehensive study of the new ideas and practices that are emerging on the shop floor must therefore lead one beyond extensive surveys, factory tours, short interview programmes, and documentary research. It must involve evidence of change as reflected in the daily routines of the shop floor itself. This is the only way to make the important link between attitudes and behaviour.

Studying the shop floor

Nowadays first hand study of the conduct of managers and workers as they meet upon the shop floor has, sadly, fallen out fashion. This is a surprising turn of events given that workplace ethnographies in the past which identified and analysed the culture of particular workplaces provided a wealth of insights into management and worker behaviour (see, for example, Roy 1952, 1955; Lupton 1963; Cunninson 1966; Brown 1973; Batstone *et al.* 1977; Edwards and Scullion 1982; for a broad review, see Edwards 1992). These studies made intensive examination of management and worker interaction based on a clear and disciplined intellectual thesis. By attempting to observe and explain events within the context in which they occurred, they generated an understanding of behaviour which was premised upon the cultural perspectives of the people being studied. Workplace ethnographers were not trammelled by the need to define and subsequently test narrow hypotheses. The productiveness of their work stemmed in part from their freedom to develop a comprehension of particular phenomena as these were revealed during the course of fieldwork. The identification, portrayal and explanation of such shop floor behaviour as 'effort restriction', 'fiddles', 'custom and practice' and 'strong bargaining relationships' has played an important part in illuminating shop floor industrial relations.

The value of an ethnographic approach to workplace relations is that it can illustrate and begin to explain the complexity of social change to a degree which other research techniques cannot. But ten, twenty, and in some cases thirty years have passed since these pioneering studies were written up. Do the sorts of behaviour they describe still figure in the modern industrial workplace, or have they been superseded by new forms of conduct? What is the present day significance of such phenomena, old and new? To answer these questions one must go beyond the anecdotes that appear in newspapers and enliven the closing discussions of seminars. One must return to the shop floor and once again conduct detailed case study research. This book examines the changing nature of employment relations in modern industry by means of three detailed factory case studies, each providing a substantial account of the attitudes, behaviour and circumstances of the managers and workers concerned. It is best from the outset, however, to be clear about the sorts of generalisations or inferences which can be drawn from intensive case study research and to say something about the nature and reliability of the evidence upon which they are founded.

Generalising from case studies

It is common to encounter the view that case studies are of limited value because they illuminate only the circumstances of particular situations: one often hears the suggestion that they are unable to shed light upon the broader whole because one cannot, with any reliability, 'generalise' from a small number of instances. Yet this opinion, whilst widely held, is mistaken and based upon a narrow understanding of what it means to 'generalise' from the particular to the wider situation. Whilst it is the purpose of social surveys to count instances of particular phenomena, and make estimates of how common they are, generalising from case studies means something rather different. Not only do case studies trade breadth for depth, they offer the possibility of developing a quite different sort of insight into social behaviour. Mitchell has provided an eloquent account of the rationale for case study thinking. He says,

the inferential process turns exclusively upon the theoretically necessary linkages among features of the case study. The validity of the extrapolation depends not upon the typicality or representativeness of the case, but the cogency of the theoretical reasoning. (Mitchell 1983 p.211)

Case studies are not about indicating how common a particular phenomenon is, but rather about helping one to understand how situations come to be the way they are. In the present study, this means using the evidence of behaviour in particular enterprises to shed light upon issues which are common to a wider range of business organisations.

The relevance of the social processes unearthed by case studies depends upon how situations in which the research takes place correspond to the wider world. They can sometimes be at their most useful where they examine situations which are in some sense 'typical' of the circumstances or problem to be investigated. The case studies which form the core of this book analyse the behaviour of managers and workers in the food processing industry in Britain. Their wider relevance depends on a judgement of the degree to which the circumstances of managers and workers in the food processing plants bear some resemblance to those in large scale manufacturing industry more generally.

At first sight, the production of foodstuffs does not closely resemble the production of motor cars, mechanical components or electronic goods, which have traditionally been the absorbing interest of industrial relations commentators. Yet food processing provides employment for a considerable number of people, on a scale almost equalling the whole of mechanical engineering, slightly exceeding that of electrical and electronic engineering, and far exceeding those employed in the manufacture of motor vehicles and parts (*Employment Gazette*, August 1992). For this reason alone it is surprising that the industry has not been visited more frequently by researchers, and one might judge that further research would serve a worthwhile purpose.

The product market in which food processing firms compete has differed to some degree from that experienced by engineering manufacturers. Food processing companies did not experience the collapse in market demand at the beginning of the 1980s which stimulated rapid re-organisation in engineering. But this is not sufficient reason to consider food processing companies as 'special cases', set apart from the rest of industry as a whole. The situation of engineering was not universal and there is evidence to suggest that like many other types of modern business, the food processing industry is highly competitive. Very large companies expend considerable energy competing for a share in product markets; managers and workers work under continuous and increasing pressure to improve quality and reduce costs (Smith *et al.* 1991).

The rapid technological innovation nowadays essential for the manufacture of many electronic products is also not generally a characteristic of food production. Equally, however, expensive capital investments are a feature of the industry and companies must endeavour to continuously modernise and maximise the efficiency of their plants if they are to remain competitive. As in other industries, pressures upon the technical organisation of production are giving rise to the development of a more flexible workforce, able to undertake a broader range of tasks, and operate faster and more sophisticated machinery.

Food processing companies, like many other industrial organisations, operate in competitive markets and face the challenge of modernisation. Recognition of these factors, however, can be no more than the starting point for scholarly analysis. Co-operation at work, or the lack of it, is not determined in any simple way by the nature of the product market or the physical nature of production. Gallie (1978), for example, illustrated how the dissimilar behaviour of British and French oil refinery workers, subject to almost identical product markets and production technology, was rooted in the different cultural values which they brought to the employment relationship. Others have illustrated how aspects of organisation culture and attitudes to employment can be manipulated by particular groups within an organisation in their attempts to alter the distribution of power. For example, managers may use the threat of competition as a lever to secure shop floor acceptance of their plans, thereby inhibiting dissent (Marchington 1990). Similarly, management's choice of new technology or equipment is often greatly influenced by a desire to enhance its power over shop floor workers (Wilkinson 1983; Willman and Winch 1985; Rose *et al.* 1986). The issue, in large, mature industrial workplaces, is how managers and workers are responding to market pressures and the changing possibilities for organising work organisation. Workplace ethnography, by offering the possibility of connecting the attitudes and behaviour of managers and workers to the circumstances in which they occur, is a technique well suited for exploring such matters.

A comparative approach

In a recent review of British workplace studies Edwards concluded that a tradition of research usually concerned exclusively with one workplace has been 'comparatively weak on causal analysis and on what kinds of generalisation can be drawn' (1991b p.11). There can be little doubt that placing various case studies side by side increases the analytical power of ethnographic research very considerably. For example, Lupton (1963) compared a factory making electrical goods with one making clothes. The factories differed from each other in almost every possible respect and this enabled him to illustrate both substantial differences in workplace behaviour and speculate as to their possible cause. Lupton ascribed significance to the production system, the nature of the workforce, the nature of the product market, the scale of the industry and various other characteristics of management–worker relationships. Comparative research was taken a stage further by Edwards and Scullion (1982). Using a mixture of observation and interviews with managers and workers in a clothing firm, an engineering company, and a chemical plant, they set out to explain why some forms of behaviour arise in some workplaces rather than others.

Both these studies confirm that comparative research offers a good opportunity to contribute to our understanding of shop floor behaviour. In order to make clear comparisons, however, it can sometimes be helpful to restrict the diversity of establishments studied. For example, in Lupton's work, the comparison of workplaces with few features in common enabled him to present a series of interesting contrasts, but at the same time made it correspondingly harder to sort out a long list of possible behavioural influences into those which were most or least important. Edwards and Scullion were aware of this problem and chose instead to illustrate how the significance of various contributory influences was not independent but varied in accordance with different circumstances. Both these studies, however, presented findings from diverse workplaces because their purpose was to document and explain the general diversity of shop floor behaviour.

The purpose of this book is different. Here, the issue is not how a variety of different circumstances have shaped workplace behaviour, but rather how different approaches to the management of industrial relations have fared on the shop floor of large manufacturing enterprises. For this reason, the cases which form the core of this book display diverse patterns of industrial relations but were deliberately chosen on account of the similarity in their operating environment and physical characteristics. Each of the case study establishments was owned by large multi-national companies and they each mass-produced foodstuffs for a similar market dominated by large retailers with considerable purchasing power. Profit margins and delivery deadlines were tight, and repeat orders depended upon timely delivery of goods. Although the products of each factory were different, the physical process of production was broadly similar, relying on large scale process technology followed by high speed mechanical wrapping of finished products. Each factory employed more than 1,000 workers and was a mature organisation, having existed for thirty years or more.

Since these broad contextual features of product markets and production technologies were common to each case, they cannot be held to account for each company's quite different approach to labour relations. As chapters 3–5 show, at the frozen food works management had traditionally pursued an adversarial approach, continuously attempting to limit unwanted union influence on the shop floor. Management at the biscuit works, however, had deliberately brought about union recognition and encouraged membership, intentionally making the union part of managing the works. In the third of the factories, a chocolate works, management had, as a matter of policy, managed without unions since the factory was founded.

Other features of the factories studied in chapters 3–5 would, no doubt, have been of interest to researchers in other fields of social enquiry but were beyond the scope of this study. The food processing industry as a whole employs large numbers of women, and this was reflected in the workforce of each factory. A substantial proportion of the workforce at both the chocolate works and the biscuit works was also drawn from various ethnic minorities. To date, other studies have done much to illuminate the working experiences of women (see, for example, Pollert 1981; Cavendish 1982; Westwood 1983). Undoubtedly further endeavour in bringing to light the employment experience of women and ethnic minorities would add to our understanding of work and society. But it is important to draw a clear distinction between analysis of shop floor relations and other kinds of issues (Edwards 1987 pp.263–269). For this study, the relevance of gender and ethnicity was considered only in terms of their influence upon patterns of shop floor behaviour. This has long been the established approach in workplace ethnography. For example, Lupton (1963), Cunninson (1966), Millward (1972) and Edwards and Scullion (1982) all studied workplaces where a substantial proportion of those employed were female. Each of these studies advanced the view that differences in shop floor behaviour were the result of differences in patterns of authority. Similarly, at the chocolate works and the biscuit works, the composition of the workforce is analysed only in terms of its contribution to shop floor behaviour.

Fieldwork

Organisation

Fieldwork was conducted at the three plants continuously between September 1986 and August 1987, dividing the total of eleven months unequally between them. Approximately 50 percent of the time was spent at the chocolate works, a further 30 percent at the biscuit works, and the remaining 20 percent at the frozen food works.

The reasons for apportioning fieldwork in this way reflected a mixture of pragmatism and opportunism. The chocolate company granted very generous access to managers, employees and documentation. Since relatively little has been written about experiences of British workers and managers in large non-union establishments this was too good an opportunity to miss. On more pragmatic grounds, it also took much longer to become accustomed to this situation because life on the shop floor possessed few features normally associated with British industrial relations. During the first few weeks of fieldwork, the chocolate works presented a puzzling picture. In place of the traditional rituals of consultation and bargaining with elected worker representatives which have characterised most other accounts of shop floor behaviour, there was a clear and self-conscious management style. Senior individuals within the organisation were unwilling to recognise any distinction between managers and other employees. To the newcomer, company life appeared to revolve around a common uniform and canteen, generous terms and conditions, and clear policies for handling grievances. Getting used to these new symbols, and finding out what they meant to different people, took some considerable time. For some time, all attempts to make sense of field notes ended in the frustrated belief that apart from details of clear management policy, they were otherwise simply a record of 'gossip' between individuals. It was not until later that it became clear that in an environment in which there were no elected worker representatives, 'gossip' was a profoundly important form of communication.

At the biscuit works and the frozen food works, the management of industrial relations revolved around well developed structures of work-place representation and it took less time to get used to the field. In the early stages of the research, management–union discussions were not only of interest in themselves, but provided a key to broader workplace issues. Nonetheless, both of these studies presented their own challenges. At the biscuit works, the relationship between the management and the union, and the support which the latter drew from the shop floor, was puzzling throughout the time spent at the factory. At the frozen food works, changes were being introduced in an environment which had previously been marked by antagonism and well-organised industrial action. On the one hand, the tense atmosphere which resulted from production levels consistently falling below management expectations made fieldwork more difficult, as what little trust existed between managers and workers soon evaporated. On the other hand, the strong emotions which were aroused by a transition from one method of working to another led to forthright expression of views, making fieldwork easier.

Conducting the case studies concurrently, making regular visits to each plant throughout the eleven months of fieldwork, had both advantages and disadvantages. On the one hand, by reducing the amount of time it was possible to spend continuously in the workplace, people may have become even more aware of 'a stranger in their midst'. On the other hand, by spreading out fieldwork over a longer period of time, it was easier to trace the development of issues and to understand how change took place. Since this was an important part of the purpose of this study, the balance of advantage lay with concurrent visits.

Evidence

Ethnographers of the shop floor enjoy the considerable benefit of being able to entertain and evaluate many different sorts of evidence. Yet by the same token they have sometimes been criticised for being unwilling to be guided by 'hard evidence' in reaching conclusions. One aspect of this criticism is directed at ethnographers' reticence in developing measures of productivity and explaining changes in those measures. In reply to such criticism, one might argue that the narrow emphasis upon productivity which has characterised the work of some industrial economists may have tended to obscure more about British industrial relations than it has revealed. Moreover, one might contend that on closer inspection productivity measures have not constituted the reliable or 'hard' evidence that others suppose to be the case. All too often what has purported to be 'hard evidence' has been unable to withstand close scrutiny (Nichols 1986). During the fieldwork for this study, in the course of attempts to piece together the often limited available data in this respect, not only did one become aware that accounting practices differed greatly between firms, but also that figures were produced by management for a variety of different purposes.

The meaning which managers give to the idea of productivity is also more complicated than commonly supposed. Ahlstrand (1990) illustrated how managers who were in possession of a surfeit of productivity statistics maintained a twenty year long commitment to the manifestly ineffective practice of productivity bargaining on account of other broader organisational values and goals. Baldamus (1961), Lupton (1963), and Guest (1990), to name but three, have all argued that managers' evaluation of workers' effort depends to a considerable extent upon their own subjective criteria. Similarly, observation and discussions with managers during this study suggested that they often regarded changes in output or productivity as dependent upon many factors, including the commitment of employees. In practice, it was impossible to distinguish alterations in productivity which were due to changes in workers' effort from those which occurred as a result of other changes in the plant or the equipment. For these reasons, the concept of productivity does not figure in the analysis presented in chapters 3–5.

The strength of particular case studies depends not upon an all too dubious distinction between 'hard' and 'soft' evidence, but upon the ways in which various kinds of evidence are used to answer particular questions. Still further criticism has been made, however, about the level of proof obtainable in ethnographic research. The difficulty of replicating studies has laid ethnographers open to the charge that their efforts are a subjective account because they cannot be repeated and confirmed by independent means. This standard of proof is, however, not always possible or universally applied even in experimental science. Nor is it the sole criterion by which scientific enquiry should be judged. Ethnographers generally ascertain the validity of their findings by comparing data from different sources. And since ethnographic studies are generally presented to an audience who themselves have firsthand experience of similar field situations, collection and interpretation of data is generally subject to informed criticism. In any event, such criticisms of ethnographic research must surely be weighed alongside the limitations of possible alternatives.

Seeking the views of managers and workers through other means is, by comparison, likely to place restrictions upon the issues which the researcher can explore. Although attitude surveys by means of structured and self-administered questionnaires permit statements of quantifiable precision, it is often impossible to ask detailed questions about sensitive issues; the way in which questions are written can exercise an important effect on responses; and the imposition of pre-coded replies upon respondents can obscure important details. Alternatively, anyone who has tried to organise a series of structured interviews within a factory will be aware of the difficulties they cause for production: it is rarely possible to talk to workers or managers for long enough to be able to overcome a sense of formality and occasion.

In this respect, the flexibility of ethnography scores above other methods. During fieldwork, the ethnographer is not testing hypotheses but becoming sensitised to a variety of new issues beyond those initially imagined (Glaser and Strauss 1968; Hammersley 1990). By spending a considerable period within the factory, one has greater opportunity to correct any erroneous first impressions and prejudices associated with being a complete newcomer to the shop floor community. And even when structured data is collected alongside unstructured data, one often finds that the effective interpretation of the former depends upon intimate knowledge of the workplace culture. The validity of ethnographic data is therefore more appropriately judged not by whether or not it can be replicated, but rather by the care with which it is collected and analysed:

observation, correctly undertaken, means that actors speak for themselves, in their normal situation . . . it encourages a continual comparison of statements in different situations. (Batstone *et al.* 1977 p.170)

Careful data collection and analysis involve procedures which allow rival interpretations to compete for a degree of empirical support. It is this which enables ethnographic accounts to withstand rigorous examination. The task in hand is therefore, 'disciplined examination rather than moral condemnation' (Gouldner 1955 p.11). Allowing workers to 'speak for themselves in their normal situation' makes it possible to capture and interpret data with a degree of subtlety not afforded by other techniques.

Some ethnographers have believed that the best way to understand the culture of an organisation is to become a functioning part of that organisation. For this reason, Roy (1952, 1955) and Burawoy (1979) became operators in the machine shop they studied. On account of this Roy was able to explain, in great detail, both the context and the rationality with which workers restricted output. Similarly Burawoy was able to describe vividly how he was sucked into the process of 'making out'. By getting so close to his subjects, Roy believed that the 'experimental' approach of the human relations movement had misrepresented and patronised workers. Burawoy's proximity to the shop floor enabled him to explain how joint procedures for handling grievances served to reconcile workers to their employment and ultimately to capitalism.

Despite the wealth of insight which participant observation can provide, however, it would not have been helpful to adopt the role of production worker in this study. It is difficult to reconcile a continuous comparison of different plants with participant observation. Most jobs in modern factories require a degree of proficiency only gained through practice. Regular absences from work and incompetence do not make for easy relations with would-be colleagues. In addition, a participant in the production process often has to accept a view of workplace relations restricted to the immediate vicinity of a particular job. Roy (1970) himself recognised that participant observation can become inconvenient where parties may engage in conflict. Talking to managers, asking awkward or impertinent questions, becomes more difficult when one is a participant in production.

For these reasons, it was preferable not to assume a temporary identity. In the situations studied most people seemed to believe that students need an education in life, and were prepared to share their own experiences of work. Equally, however, most university students eventually find jobs as managers rather than researchers, and this made some people suspicious of what purpose the research might serve (an interesting reaction in itself given that advocates of the 'new industrial relations' have claimed that it is able to overcome perceptions of divided interests). Even participant observers, however, whose aim is to immerse themselves in the culture of an organisation, cannot avoid the problems of presenting a particular identity. Where bonuses and promotions are available, where good jobs are allocated to some people and bad ones to others, then the researcher's behaviour inevitably changes respondents' conduct. In truth, it is impossible for a researcher to avoid having some impact on the field and it is hard to know how the conduct of this research altered the way people behaved. For the most part, however, one might judge that their behaviour was shaped by influences far stronger than the presence of a single researcher on the shop floor.

The first few weeks of fieldwork in each plant were spent finding out how production was organised. An initial interest in 'how the job is done' provided an opportunity to make introductions to the shop floor with apparently factual questions. Thereafter, as it became possible to get to know individual workers better, so discussions included issues which workers regarded as being more sensitive. At the chocolate works, a good deal of time was spent with one particular shift. By staying with them and following their fortunes it became easier to generate a degree of mutual understanding. Throughout fieldwork, paying close attention to the way in which jobs changed, how staff numbers varied, and how managers behaved on the shop floor, yielded rewarding insights.

In each factory, observation and shop floor discussions with both individuals and groups of workers were supplemented by 'depth interviews' with members of management and, where they were present, shop stewards. In the course of extensive and repeated discussions, structured to varying degrees, they would recount their version of what was happening in the factory and why things were turning out in particular ways. Slowly but surely, these interviews made it possible to establish a chronology of significant events, and understand more about how managers and workers regarded each other. Most interviews were conducted within the plant. On a few occasions it was useful to interview people formerly employed at the plant, some of whom subsequently worked at more senior levels of management. These individuals provided a broader view of company policies, as well as interesting accounts of how industrial relations had been managed in the past.

There are clear difficulties in understanding the past by means of personal recollections and reflections. Memory is often inaccurate, selective and bound up with judgement: individual accounts of history sometimes serve not as a faithful record of events but as justification of personal involvement. There are, however, few alternatives to this kind of information. Business organisations are not archives and usually few written records of value exist. Information is often destroyed or incomplete, remaining only in people's memories. In such circumstances the practice adopted has been, wherever possible, to compare accounts from different points of view rather than to rely upon the recollection of a single person.

Towards the end of fieldwork, evidence from informal discussions and observation was supplemented by some quantitative evidence of the extent to which workers shared opinions of their employment. To confirm the generality of certain views emerging from discussions with individuals, a short self-completion questionnaire was issued to workers in those departments where observation and interviews had been conducted. Self-completion questionnaires tend to pre-judge the range of workers' replies, but they can serve as a means of canvassing a large number of workers in confidence. Questionnaires were distributed and collected in sealed envelopes in person. In each workplace they drew a satisfactory response rate; at the biscuit works 190 questionnaires were returned from lines which employed a total of approximately 300 people; at the chocolate works, a similar proportion of workers responded, 155 questionnaires being returned from lines employing around 230 people. At the frozen food works, although management was unwilling to allow meat workers the opportunity to express their feelings on paper (for reasons which will become all too apparent in later chapters), the questionnaire was issued to other workers included in the study. It drew a considerable response; 104 questionnaires were returned from a line which employed 115 people. The results proved useful in gaining a broader measure of the strength of feeling on particular issues. Details of the attitude surveys are provided in each of the following case study chapters.

Two years after fieldwork at the frozen food works had ended, an opportunity arose to attend conciliation meetings between the management and the union in the course of an industrial dispute. During this process, which lasted several days, it was possible to watch the exchanges which took place between management and unions in joint meetings, and to talk to each party individually in side meetings. Observing the conciliation process provided a fascinating illustration of the parties' relationship and the way it was coping (or otherwise) with the stresses imposed by change.

Some time has passed since fieldwork was completed. In part, pressures of other work account for the delay in publishing these studies. But it has also taken some considerable time to reach a clear understanding of what was happening in each of the organisations. In the time that has elapsed it is likely that certain things have changed, but broadly speaking the conclusions are still likely to be valid. The conciliation meetings between the managers and workers of the frozen food works made it clear that the issues identified earlier had not gone away: if anything, they had become more acute.

The following chapters tell an interesting story about the way in which industrial relations may be changing in major parts of manufacturing industry. They afford an opportunity to examine how shop floor relations are adapting to competitive pressures. To date, many accounts of modernisation have concentrated upon developments in the exceptional situations of 'greenfield' establishments, in which social relationships are less encumbered by history (see, for example, Geary 1992a, 1992b). In contrast, this study takes a look at how large and mature industrial enterprises are coping with change.

In each of the following cases, it is possible to see in management's approach to industrial relations some of the typical problems and issues which have figured in the writings of British industrial relations commentators. For example, at the frozen food works, relations between managers and workers had long embodied a good deal of antagonism and the degree of trust which existed between them was very limited. Their relations had for many years resulted in the sorts of adversarial behaviour once believed to be endemic within post-war British industrial relations, but which according to some commentators had been all but eradicated by the early 1980s. At the biscuit works, the company had embraced the message of post-war reform and was determined to ensure that trades unions served to strengthen rather than weaken management prerogative. Its approach to industrial relations is an example of an orthodoxy in which so many commentators once placed their hopes for the future, but which some have since judged ineffective and outdated. At the chocolate works, the determination of management to remain free of unions suggested an individual approach to labour relations which may have since become increasingly attractive to managers in general. In these ways, the three case studies described in chapters 3–5 may be able to offer some insights into broader questions. Have adversarial attitudes been overcome? Must orthodox reform necessarily fail? Is the non-union model a possible way forward?

3   The frozen food works

Introduction

For many years, relations between managers and workers at the frozen food works had been turbulent. But, facing stiff competition, management came to the view that a new approach to industrial relations should be an integral part of a broader reorganisation of manufacturing activities. Senior managers drew up radical plans to bring about a fundamental change in the 'quality of working life', with a view to transforming adversarial relationships into co-operative ones. They sought to bring the disagreements of the past to an end by moving away from a traditional 'one person, one job' way of organising production to a system based upon autonomous work groups responsible for organising most aspects of their own work.

This chapter is an account of the introduction of new working arrangements and their consequences on the shop floor. It explores the way in which managers identified and analysed their industrial relations 'problems', and contemplates the thinking behind their new approach and how it differed from traditional management methods. The way in which the new working arrangements were practised on the shop floor is described, and their impact upon workers and their relations with managers is analysed. Workers' attitudes towards the local union, and the influence of the shop stewards upon the development of the new working practices, are also examined. Most importantly of all, however, this chapter contemplates the lack of success with which the new approach was able to resolve the disagreements between managers and workers, and illuminates the reasons for its failure to bring about more positive and productive workplace relations.

Events at the frozen food works illustrate the difficulties which management faces when introducing changes within the constraints of an existing situation. Not only was management's attitude towards change conditioned by past thinking, but workers also continued to regard management with considerable suspicion. As a consequence, the events which surrounded the commissioning of new working methods were interpreted by each party in terms of their traditional outlook and values. History had shaped a workplace culture which ran counter to the aims of reform. In spite of both management's and workers' earnest desire for change, co-operation remained elusive. In some areas of the factory, management continued to exercise prerogative in a traditionally detailed fashion; in others the extent of restrictive practices was, if anything, increased and management authority was considerably weakened. Turbulent and unsatisfactory industrial relations remained the norm.

The management approach: old problems, new ideas

The frozen food works was owned by a British subsidiary of a multinational company. It was one of several owned by the same organisation within the UK. The company had in recent years positioned an extensive product range within the quality foodstuffs market. But it faced considerable competition from other producers, and a substantial proportion of production was sold to large supermarket chains with considerable purchasing power. This particular factory made a number of frozen food products on production lines of varying sophistication. Generally speaking, on account of recent investment, it was one of the most modern and highly mechanised of the company's factories.

The company had been the largest employer of local labour for many years, employing over 2,000 people at two factories situated close to one another. Following reorganisation and automation, production was concentrated at one plant employing about 1,200 people. Responsibility for the management of industrial relations was split between an experienced local personnel manager, assisted by a training manager and a personnel officer, and the company's head office personnel function. At the time of the study, most elements of pay were negotiated on a national basis and manual workers' rates were determined within a company-wide job evaluation scheme. The local personnel manager dealt with disputes, grievances and dismissals, in the first stages of longstanding written procedures. Formally the company refused to enter into discussions about staffing levels and working practices, but in practice the local personnel manager spent much of his time on these matters. Two unions were recognised at the plant; one for unskilled and semi-skilled manuals, the other for skilled manuals. Nearly all the shop floor workers were union members and union dues were collected by means of a 'check-off' arrangement with management. This study concentrates upon unskilled and semi-skilled manual workers, who were represented by nine shop stewards, most of whom were chosen by means of contested elections. The majority of the stewards had several years' experience. Those with the longest service tended to be elected to the 'negotiations committee' which was chaired by a full time convenor, for whom management provided an office and administrative facilities on site. In all these respects, the institutional arrangements for industrial relations had come to resemble those found in many large manufacturing workplaces.

The company expanded rapidly throughout the 1950s and 1960s to a point where it had achieved market dominance and made substantial profits. But whilst senior managers concentrated upon meeting the demands of a fast-growing market, the development of company-wide policies for industrial relations was given low priority and, by all accounts, industrial relations developed in a diverse and 'disorderly' way. Like many British employers, responsibility for industrial relations matters lay with local factory managers (Donovan 1968, para 83–95). Sometimes they sought the advice of Head Office, but on most matters they were free to arrive at whatever local, and often informal, arrangements they felt necessary.

Several unions organised all of the company's six plants and bargaining thrived in nearly sixty sets of local, annual, wage negotiations. But the consequence of these increasingly complex ad hoc arrangements was mounting disorder as, according to senior management, discrepancies in wage rates and working practices between plants provoked a large number of disputes. By the beginning of the 1970s the company, concerned that management prerogative was being steadily weakened by an ever-growing regime of custom and practice, set out to eliminate opportunities for its development. They established company-wide negotiations on all major aspects of terms and conditions, and a company-wide job evaluation scheme. Senior managers at Head Office also tried to strengthen the resolve of local management by encouraging them to impose a tough policy on shop floor discipline. Known within management as 'Work or want', it declared that workers must obey a supervisor's instruction within 15 minutes, making any objection through the grievance procedure, or face suspension without pay. The policy was a bold attempt to change a situation from one in which the status quo prevailed to one in which management prerogative could be enforced in the first instance. In effect, 'Work or want' was the equivalent of management saying that it did not require agreement before implementing decisions.

According to managers, recourse to 'macho management' did not do the trick. Custom and practice continued to thrive and several long strikes took place. Ten years later, at the beginning of the 1980s, senior management once again found it necessary to launch a fundamental reform of working practices. Taking stock of its existing industrial relations senior company officials felt that there was significant over-staffing, that many workers did not work efficiently, and that they enjoyed unacceptable amounts of 'idle time'.

Senior head office management came to the view that the company's own management style was partly to blame for poor performance. They said that conservative management attitudes had fostered an environment in which management was predominantly 'concerned with being right' in the smallest of decisions. And there was too much 'little management' practised by 'warders, meddlers, and nannies' (senior management briefing paper, circa 1984). To put things right, senior management declared that there should be a new management style which should not simply coerce workers into obeying management decisions, but rather improve their motivation by obliging them to take responsibility for making some of those decisions themselves:

People like to work and want to work and produce their best efforts only when they are allowed to have some control over their work. (Senior management brief)

Senior management proposed that workers should be organised in autonomous teams. These teams should be given all the necessary powers of decision-making to meet production and quality targets, and be under obligation to work flexibly in order to attain them. In the words of senior management, the initiative required the company to redefine the 'existing line of demarcation between managers and managed', pulling that line 'up to the highest possible point', below which 'the allocation of responsibilities should become a matter for the group, not for management'.

At the core of the proposals for change was a belief, common to much of the thinking behind the 'new industrial relations', that if it were possible to make work more interesting workers would be better motivated to serve management goals. Senior managers also knew that for the new working practices to be effective there would have to be a transformation in the attitudes of shop floor managers and workers towards each other. To this end, they proposed that there should be many fewer supervisors. Those that remained should be concerned with assisting workers to improve their decision-making techniques, rather than with the minute direction of effort, as had been the case in the past. It was equally important that workers worked much harder than they had done before. The company believed that it was necessary to signal a clear break with the past by establishing higher standards of effort from the outset of the new approach, lest extensive 'idle time' once again become part of the accepted pattern of work:

Raw numbers and skills must be pared to the minimum possible before the new working practices are allowed to emerge. This is a straightforward, hard-headed management exercise and a tough task for the industrial relations negotiators.

Whilst management recognised that its own approach had contributed to poor relations, it also identified the power of shop stewards as a substantial barrier to progress. The company regarded the shop stewards as the cause of inadequate effort and believed that the key to higher standards of effort in future was their exclusion from discussions about work organisation. In future, managers should directly persuade shop floor workers of the company view, without looking to the shop stewards as intermediaries, or giving them the opportunity to argue back. Senior management declared that,

the [traditional] line of communication must be changed if the new working practice is to have any chance at all.

In the new scheme of things, therefore, management wanted to reduce the influence of trades unions in shop floor decision-making:

Their [trades unions] function is to negotiate terms and conditions on which their members are prepared to work. It is not to interfere with the business, ... or the means of production, ... The factory general managers will say how they want to run their factories. The trades unions will negotiate the price.

Senior management also encouraged local managers to stand firm in possible arguments over work standards. The new management style demanded that they should be 'decisive in conflict', bringing disputes to a head quickly and winning them outright. 'Second-best' compromises, or illicit deals designed to buy temporary co-operation in return for a relaxation of standards, were no longer permissible.

Management's vision of the future was an eclectic mixture of modern thinking and traditional company attitudes. On the one hand the new approach laid stress upon developing fulfilling work routines and open relationships between workers and supervisors, but on the other it advocated a tough unilateral approach to discipline and effort. The new approach granted workers greater autonomy in the performance of their tasks, in the belief that it was essential for achieving high standards of motivation, but at the same time prevented them using it in ways contrary to management intentions. Management placed enormous faith in the view that a more varied and interesting work routine would enable employees to identify more readily with company goals and enhance their motivation and effort, but at the same time insisted upon uncompromising mainten- ance of its prerogative. These paradoxes betrayed the extent to which management's thinking continued to be suffused by its judgement as to the persistent problem of the past thirty years, namely the 'unco-operative' behaviour of shop stewards. In developing the new working arrangements there was, as far as one can tell, little understanding of why the shop stewards had, in some areas, developed and maintained enormous influence upon shop floor behaviour. Management's only answer was to continue with the assertion that their behaviour was 'illegal'. Just as in the past, it believed that vigorous exclusion of the union from discussions about routine changes in working practices would dissipate the traditional adversarial climate and make workers more amenable to persuasion in favour of the company view. How was this cocktail of old and new thinking implemented upon the shop floor?

Preparations for change

Prior to the new arrangements the company embarked upon a major re-organisation and refitting of the works. The investment totalled many millions of pounds, expanded plant capacity and created a substantial number of new jobs. It was announced that the other local factory, which management judged to have an appalling labour relations record, would be closed, with considerable job losses.

The company intended that this re-organisation should make a clean break with the past and establish new standards of effort. Re-design of production facilities offered opportunities to achieve lean staffing, and management intended to reshape the workforce by offering employment only to the most able and motivated employees, selected from the labour force of each plant. But these opportunities proved hard to realise. At the factory due for closure, the union called a nation-wide strike over the redundancy terms offered by the company. Through well organised picketing of distribution depots, it prevented the delivery of products to shops and supermarkets with great effectiveness. Management quickly returned to negotiations, agreed to reduce the number of proposed redundancies, and forfeited its right to select workers for future employ-ment by instead heeding the traditional principle of 'last-in-first out'. Workers with the longest experience of 'Work or want' therefore became those employed under the new initiative. Well organised union activity had shaped the course of change to a remarkable degree, even in circumstances of redundancies and plant closure where workers' economic power is often judged to be weak. And by giving way on these matters, the company's first attempts to shape new work standards enjoyed only limited success. In practice, it had proved much more difficult than management had anticipated to use the threat of selective redundancies and unemployment to establish a new standard of effort.

Although the company put forward the new initiative in part with the aim of reducing the influence of trades unions, it knew that it could not make progress without their co-operation. Local management set up a joint working party of managers and senior shop stewards to discuss the nature of the proposed changes. The joint working party commissioned an opinion survey of employees, seeking their views on such matters as group working and changes in the supervision of work. Details of work organisation were put forward by working parties comprising managers and stewards from within particular departments, and these were then passed to the working party of senior representatives for approval.

It was formally agreed that work groups should make their own decisions about work allocation within their areas of responsibility and that they would be encouraged to be flexible within a range of tasks assigned to their group; they should be responsible for meeting quality standards; they should allocate overtime amongst themselves; and they should be prepared to cover for unexpected sickness or absence within their department.

Clocking on and off at the beginning and end of each shift was abolished. In accordance with the spirit of self-organisation, workers were made responsible for regulating their own attendance and were 'on trust' to establish continuous running through 'baton' shift changes. Regular off-line face to face meetings would take place between supervisors and workers to discuss improvements in output and quality. In return for these changes, it was also agreed that all workers in a particular department would be paid at the same rate and in addition would be given a five pounds a week supplement for extra responsibilities. For many workers, the combined effect of their jobs being regraded and the payment of the new responsibility allowance was a substantial wage increase.

At the end of their extensive discussions, management and unions judged that they had made considerable progress. Management believed that the new working practices would eliminate the demarcation and restrictions of the past and prevent new restrictive practices arising in future. The union believed it had secured considerable wage increases and improvements in working conditions for its members. But with hindsight, the consequences were rather more complicated and well illustrate the fact that when planning change, managers rarely start from a blank sheet of paper: instead, they often have to work within the political constraints of an existing situation.

Although management intended that shop stewards should be excluded from future detailed discussions on changes in work organisation, it had little choice but to involve the union in the design of the new working practices; it knew that change would not be accepted on the shop floor without union approval. But management's dependence upon union co-operation inhibited frank discussion about how the role of shop stewards should be reformed. Consequently, the new agreements specified working practices in considerable detail, but said very little about management prerogatives or the appropriate behaviour of shop stewards. Management had not agreed to a redefinition of the role of supervisors or the permissible limits of autonomous work group decision-making. Nor had shop stewards assented to a reduction in their influence over these matters. As a result, despite extensive bargaining and consultation about the details of the new working arrangements, there was considerable scope for different under-standings to develop about the principles involved in coping with unforeseen situations. Additionally, extensive consultation and discussion with the workforce had inevitably led workers to form high expectations of the benefits of change. Agreement was therefore more limited than it appeared, and the extent to which management and workers understood what was expected of each other was open to doubt. These different understandings played an important part in the way in which the future unfolded.

Workers' reactions to change (1)

The new working practices were first introduced into a small department of the factory which employed about 120 people in the processing of vegetables. It had the reputation of being an easy department to manage. Management felt that workers who had been relatively co-operative in the past would respond positively to the changes, getting them off to a good start. And so they did, up to a point.

Under the new working arrangements work was divided between four self-regulating groups of workers. The first group was responsible for checking the quality of incoming raw materials; the second group was responsible for the operation of the process plant; the third group operated the packaging equipment and delivered finished products to the warehouse; the fourth group fed conveyor belts to the packing line, and undertook final quality inspection. In the first and second groups, workers were called upon to make decisions and adjustments which had significant bearing upon the quality of the finished product. Their discretion and experience was important, but they were not always continuously employed. If things were going smoothly they might not have much to do. In the third and fourth groups, however, workers' efforts were much more closely tied to the speed at which the packaging machinery operated. They were more or less continuously employed and their work offered them less scope for making fine judgements. Within each of the work groups, successful production required workers to work together closely as a team. Two supervisors also worked in the department and had general responsibility of co-ordinating the efforts between groups.

A year and a half after changes were implemented in the department, several weeks were spent observing the new working practices in action and talking to workers and supervisors. Nearly all of the workers expressed

Table 3.1 *How do you feel about the following features of the new working practices, compared to the way you worked before?*

row % of respondents	a lot better	a bit better	a bit worse	a lot worse
No clocking	94	5	1	0
Organising your own breaks	75	22	2	1
Job rotation	70	24	6	0
Everybody on the same pay rate	81	8	4	7
				N = 96

Table 3.2 *Since the introduction of the new working practices, do you feel your job has become more or less interesting/enjoyable?*

row % of respondents			
a lot more interesting /enjoyable	a bit more interesting /enjoyable	a bit less interesting /enjoyable	a lot less interesting /enjoyable
32	50	8	10
30	53	12	5
			N = 96

their satisfaction with the way things had changed. Tables 3.1 and 3.2 show that the great majority of workers enjoyed aspects of autonomy and clearly felt that it made their jobs more interesting and enjoyable.

Most workers also believed that the new working arrangements enabled them to enjoy friendly and constructive relations within and between work groups. Nearly all (95 percent) workers believed that other members of their work group were 'very helpful' or 'fairly helpful' in providing them with assistance and two thirds (66 percent) said other work groups were similarly helpful in providing such assistance when they needed it.

The new working practices were therefore, by any standards, successful in promoting harmonious relations amongst workers. By fostering a climate of positive relations between them, one might even suggest that they

Table 3.3 *Do members of your work group ever do any of the following?*

row % of respondents	Yes	No
Tell supervisors how well we can do our jobs	14	86
Make sure we work hard	22	78
Keep an eye on the length of our tea breaks	40	60
		$N = 92$

encouraged the development of 'team spirit'. But although 'team spirit' was a pre-requisite of successful production, enhanced motivation and effort depended upon team members encouraging one another in behaviour which would realise management goals. Within and between work groups, however, peer pressures of this sort did not develop.

Table 3.3 shows that very few workers believed that their colleagues passed information to supervisors about their competence or ensured that they worked hard. And there were no discernible differences of view on either of these matters between any of the work groups. The issue of tea breaks, however, requires more detailed consideration. Whereas only about one fifth of workers in the process and materials handling jobs believed their colleagues kept an eye on their time away from the line, around half of workers in the packaging jobs felt that their colleagues put them under pressure to get back from tea on time. At first sight this might suggest that work groups differed in their level of motivation; but a more plausible explanation of this difference between work groups has to do with the fact that workers operating packaging machinery were machine paced, whereas workers in other groups were not under the same immediate pressures.

Workers in the packaging groups who took longer breaks than their colleagues placed extra burdens upon other members of their work groups and interfered with the relief rota which the work group agreed amongst themselves. Consequently, in much the same way as workers under piecework often fix informal standards of effort, the packaging workers regulated their breaks to even out the allocation of effort and leisure within the work group. Their behaviour reflected a collective desire for equity of effort within the group, rather than a collective drive to maximise group effort. This phenomenon was a general feature of shop floor relations. Workers tended to value their good relations with colleagues so highly that they structured their obligations towards one another in ways which avoided placing strain upon their friendships. They preferred not to ask for assistance for fear of placing extra burdens on members of their group. Similarly they took a limited view of obligations to their colleagues and, by the same token, to the company. According to workers, good working relations meant not asking for help too often:

At the end of the day you have to get on with people . . . people aren't happy about being dragged from tea early. They expect you to sort out the problem for yourself. (Worker)

From the supervisors' point of view,

The problem is that you've got above and below average and they've all decided to rotate round the jobs. The above average soon pick it up, but the below average don't. When they've been off something for a few weeks they forgot what they'd learnt first time round. We had to say to them 'for Christ's sake sort yourselves out, there's two duffers on that machine – you'll have to put somebody else a bit better on with them. They didn't want to do that. If a couple of good blokes could milk the job they were on, they wouldn't give a toss if a couple of other blokes were struggling like hell. (Supervisor)

The preservation of co-operative relations within work groups therefore meant keeping demands upon colleagues to a minimum. Management was right in the belief that the new working arrangements would make work more interesting and enjoyable for workers, but wrong to believe that this would, in itself, lead to their becoming more motivated or committed to management goals.

At an early stage in the new working practices, management became somewhat dissatisfied with their results and noticed a downward drift in workers' effort. Workers had developed the habit of starting late, leaving early and spending longer on breaks in the canteen:

We've worked out how to run the place differently. So we're taking longer breaks which are justified because everything is running all right. But the supervisors don't like to see it. They've told us there shouldn't be more than six people in the canteen at once. We said, 'why grumble?' and they said 'the floor wasn't washed enough'. (Worker)

As the weeks went on, workers increased their leisure time away from the line and their 'short-cuts' became more extensive and widespread. Management claimed that bad shift changes were causing up to two hours' worth of lost production every day and increased the number of supervisors on each shift, instructing them to tighten-up on work discipline and increase output. Supervisors duly appeared much more frequently on the shop floor and things came to a head one day when the packaging line was short of staff. The shop steward told the process operators to slow down the

Table 3.4 *In your own experience of the new working practices so far, do you think that supervisors have more or less control over the following, in comparison with the way you worked before?*

row % of respondents	more control	less control	no change
Pace of output	19	31	50
Quality control	12	35	53
Discipline	3	37	60
Job allocation	1	73	26
Overtime allocation	2	69	29
Machine adjustment	19	38	43

$N = 95$

production process to avoid generating a backlog of work. The supervisors intervened quickly to return the machine to its previous speed. One of them explained,

I was mad – he shouldn't touch the machine speeds. In the end we had a reasonable chat and he said 'point taken, shan't touch it any more'. (Supervisor)

Management therefore intervened quickly to prevent a precedent which would allow the shop steward to exercise control over work. Despite having given workers' autonomy to manage their own work, when their efforts fell short of management expectations the company re-asserted its right to manage. Within a few weeks the supervisors believed that their interventions had clawed back most of the 'bad habits' that had developed. Table 3.4 shows that workers agreed with them.

Workers were not inclined to the view that the new working practices had given supervisors more control over the major aspects of their work. But in only two respects, job allocation and overtime allocation, did the majority of workers believe the influence of supervisors had been reduced. In every other aspect of work, most workers said that supervisors' influence had been unaltered. Despite the introduction of new working practices, workers believed that supervisors retained their influence in the management of production:

Recently the supervisors are always up your arse. One of them was down here on the floor for seven hours the other night ... they don't make any difference ... they just piddle about. Somebody brought it up at the consultative meeting the other week. The supervisors stayed off the line for a day but then they were back. (Worker)

Yet when the vegetable supervisors were instructed to 'tighten-up', they were apprehensive. Although management had told them to be 'decisive in conflict' they felt that the new working practices had undermined their authority and they didn't want to push their luck:

In the old days the supervisor could go in and sort something out. You took a chance, knowing that management would back you – right or wrong. So would personnel. Now if you did anything wrong you wonder whether they would support you. There's many a time I count to ten and say to myself, 'I mustn't rock the boat'. (Supervisor)

They felt it prudent to be cautious. The personnel director had visited the plant shortly before the new working practices began, in order to emphasise that the commitment of everybody was vital to their success. His visit made a big impression on the supervisors who recalled,

he said it was up to us to make it work, and if we didn't we'd get the chop. (Supervisor)

They often reflected upon the fate of their former boss. Being 'a manager of the old school', he had rather unwisely made no secret of his view that the new working practices would fail to deliver, and was fired. Thereafter the supervisors frequently talked about 'a lack of openness and trust' between themselves and their superiors. They believed that in the long term a reduction in their numbers was inevitable and anyone whose 'commitment' might be questioned on account of some reckless intervention ran the risk of losing his job. Production levels slipped, workers spent too long in the canteen, but the supervisors awaited express instruction from management before they did anything about it. Above all, it was important not to 'rock the boat', not to be seen as the cause of conflict. The supervisors became less interested in supervising and instead committed themselves to self-preservation.

Workers in the vegetable department confirmed that the supervisors had adopted a low-key approach since the introduction of the new working practices. They thought it was an improvement:

The supervisors don't tear you off a strip. They appreciate there will be cock-ups but they just have a quiet word. It's not like the old days – they used to be dictatorial. (Worker)

But at the same time, even though three fifths (60 per cent) of workers held the view that supervisors no longer had a proper role under the new working practices, and three quarters (75 per cent) believed there were too many supervisors, one of them explained,

we just do as we're told. If they [the supervisors] come up and say, 'I think you should be running this faster', you just do it because it isn't worth the hassle. Supervisors do the talking and they don't ask what you think. (Worker)

Workers accepted that supervisors had the right to set standards and give instructions so long as they were not too heavy handed about it. When the supervisors tried to make them spend more time on the line and less time in the canteen, they found it difficult to produce counter-arguments. Instead they admitted that their own behaviour had been unreasonable. Their 'short-cuts', working out how to run the place with fewer people, were in their own estimation, 'abusing the system'. People were, 'just trying to see what they could get away with', and when the supervisors tightened-up workers tended to believe that management was within its rights, even if the tighter regime did make work marginally less pleasant.

Taking these things together, it seems that the new working practices were appreciated by workers because they provided choices previously unavailable to them. Workers felt that freedom from clocking on and off, a degree of autonomy in the allocation of jobs and overtime, and more interesting, enjoyable, and better paid work were all positive improvements that stemmed directly from the new way of working. The new approach also allowed them to maintain friendly and positive relations with their workmates and enabled them to arrange their duties in order to increase their leisure time. To this extent, it seems that group working did result in 'team spirit'. But it did not encourage work teams to make greater identification with company aims. 'Peer pressure' did not develop in the way management hoped because workers were not persuaded to alter their attitudes and behaviour in ways which were more favourable to the company. Consequently management instructed supervisors to exercise traditional prerogatives once more, in order to achieve production targets. Workers accepted this increased measure of discipline without much objection, for the new working practices still allowed some valued freedoms and because the supervisors generally went about their work in an unobtrusive way. In short, the shop floor responded to the new working practices neither by accepting greater responsibility for raising production, nor by rejecting management's right to control. Instead co-operation in the department was rooted in a much older mutual understanding of the status quo.

Workers' reactions to change (2)

Shortly after the commencement of new working practices in the vegetable department, they were introduced in another department making meat products. The production process was broadly similar, and a similar pattern of work organisation was agreed which divided tasks between four teams on each of six production lines. In total, about 300 workers were employed in this part of the factory.

Management knew that it would be much harder to make the new practices work well here. Meat products had traditionally been associated with the most difficult labour relations in the company. An experiment with autonomous group working on a meat line several years earlier had ended in a strike which lasted five weeks. From the company's point of view, difficulties over the new working practices began even before they got started. The company intended to pay the meat workers the same rate as workers in the vegetable department so that there would be a single rate of pay for nearly all semi-skilled operators throughout the factory. But the meat workers refused to take part in the new working practices unless all their jobs were graded at the highest rate previously paid for any job done under the old working practices. Their argument was that if they were expected to be continuously flexible they should be paid a rate appropriate to the most complicated tasks they might have to undertake. The company was reluctant to accept their argument at first, but when the meat workers backed up this demand with an overtime ban, managers succumbed to the pressure which the company placed upon them for continuous production, and quickly gave in to workers' demands.

There were problems from the outset. Management decided to put extra supervisors on the lines and gave them instructions to improve production levels and bring about changes in working practices wherever necessary. The supervisors tried to persuade workers to spend longer on each job and thereby reduce the rate at which members of each work group changed tasks. But since workers believed that they had been given an assurance that there would be only one supervisor working in the department, they regarded management's decision to increase their number, taken without consultation, with deep suspicion. In private, some workers admitted that certain of their colleagues were not up to doing particular jobs. But they feared that the supervisors had been instructed by management to assess their competence with a view to keeping individuals in jobs to which they were best suited, and thereafter reimposing tight control over work. Disillusionment quickly set in:

The new working practices are just a sham – things are going back to the old way of working. Supervisors keep interfering. They want to put certain people in certain jobs, they're here to spy on us . . . it's just the same old story. If a machine's supposed to run at fifty an hour, this company will try to make it run at seventy five. It's always been the same for as long as I can remember. (Worker)

Workers refused to agree to the supervisors' requests and as the production difficulties remained unresolved, management accused the workers of idleness and, in reply, the workers criticised the management of incompetence and untrustworthiness. To prove their point, a good many workers recounted in some detail an incident in which a supervisor, keen to boost production, had restarted a machine, unaware that one of the operators was working inside it. Relations between supervisors and workers were characterised, not by 'a quiet word', but by talk of 'interference', 'spying' and 'selection'.

The shop stewards convened meetings on the shop floor, and in a climate of deepening fear and mistrust, co-operation became very restricted. The union argued that under the new agreement management had no right to interfere in the way groups organised their effort. Management replied that workers were rotating so quickly as to be unable to gain expertise in tasks and were therefore working inefficiently. But this cut little ice on the shop floor and the situation quickly turned sour:

They [the management] kept saying to us [the shop stewards], 'we need more tonnage, more stability in the work groups'. We had about eight or nine meetings with management, and we wouldn't budge. They said the supervisors were just there to co-ordinate, but we could see what was happening. They'd say, 'when Joe was on that machine he produced 90 tons and when Fred was on he produced only 30 tons. Let's keep Joe on and put Fred somewhere else'. That's what they were after. You can't co-ordinate without spying. Then they came out with this 'hit list'. They said, 'if you don't give us stability we'll kick out people who we think are unsuitable to work here'. We had meetings on the floor, came back to the firm and said one person taken out and we'd be out on the road. (Shop steward)

Managers laid the blame for their lack of success in part upon the allegedly malign influence of the shop stewards, accusing them of starting rumours and stirring up trouble:

You've got shop stewards in there who just don't want to see the new working practices work. It's opposite to their whole way of thinking. (Manager)

At further meetings management told the shop stewards that it would not move particular workers from their work groups. But relations between the managers and the stewards did not flourish. It was only after the intervention of the convenor that the shop stewards agreed to comply with management's request for a slower rate of task rotation. Even so, the stewards declared that further talk of 'selection' would inevitably lead to their 'withdrawing co-operation'. And their behaviour, which forced management to accept that change could be agreed 'purely on an informal basis', thereby created a precedent in which the right to alter work organisation lay with the shop floor rather than with management. Management was once again obliged to make fragile informal arrangements, undermining its own authority, in order to ensure that production continued. And once again, the shop stewards were exerting substantial influence in the informal control of work.

The stewards developed their influence still further at the expense of management by sometimes interpreting the working practices agreement to the letter. They could, when it suited them, insist on formality. Shortly after the arguments about rotation and selection had surfaced, the 'bulk box dispute' over 'extra duties' erupted on the shop floor. Management tried to persuade meat process workers to take responsibility for some extra tasks not specifically covered in the working practices agreement. The stewards refused to allow this. They judged that although the changes might initially take place only on an informal basis, they were nevertheless not in workers' interests, and would not permit any relaxation of their agreement:

The superintendent came up when one of the processes was down and asked one of the process men to fetch some bulk boxes from the cold store and feed them into the packaging system. Under our agreement we don't touch them. If a process breaks down an operator should go on training, or go and help somebody else. The superintendent said, 'I'm telling you to go and do it or I'll send you home'. The bloke said, 'no' and then the union got involved. I spoke to the superintendent and told him it wasn't part of the agreement. He kept arguing, so we had a meeting. We stopped the lines and took everybody outside. We told the superintendent that if he sent one person home, we'd all go home, and he'd lose 24 hours production. (Shop steward)

A strike seemed imminent and was only averted when the plant personnel manager conceded the issue over the heads of line management. It was formally agreed that in future extra workers would be laid on to cover the extra work.

Management's deepening disillusionment was reflected in a confidential report reviewing the operation of the new working practices in the meat department. The report alleged that the department continued to be overstaffed as operators worked a system of 'continuous relief rather than continuous production'; too many workers spent too long in the canteen and away from the production lines; 'idle-time' still permeated the work routine; 'baton' shift changes were rarely achieved because workers in the outgoing shift left early and those on the incoming shift arrived late; and certain workers had developed 'insolent' attitudes towards supervisors. The report recommended that certain unsuitable and incompetent individuals be removed from the department by 'appropriate means'. It concluded that the new working practices had failed to inspire workers and that motivation and discipline were poor. Within little more than a year of the new working practices being introduced on the meat lines, management had lost control of them. Its attempts to impose a greater measure of its authority on the shop floor had made little progress because stewards had the means to counter them with a range of threats and sanctions. The factory personnel manager admitted in private that,

the shop stewards in there have got more power than the supervisors now.

As time went on, instead of being able to by-pass the stewards, the supervisors found themselves becoming increasingly reliant upon them to organise co-operation. Trying to put a brave face on the situation, one of the department managers declared,

supervisors monitor that all procedures are maintained within the company specification. Two weeks ago we spoke to the stewards about hygiene – we gave them four weeks to get into the habit of clearing up as they went along.

The management communicated to the shop floor via the stewards, because they alleged that speaking to workers directly had little effect. A supervisor complained,

all the interest has gone out of the job for me – you can tell a group to do something but there's no saying that they'll do it.

In this way, co-operation soon came to be regulated by the shop stewards. Not only could they use the new working practices agreement to claim that management's influence over detailed aspects of work organisation was illegitimate, but they could also insist upon interpretations of the document which were most favourable to workers' interests.

Management's attempts to break away from traditional industrial relations in the meat department had little success. The new working practices did not motivate workers towards management goals and they promoted rather than prevented the development of restrictive practices. Management believed that the problems associated with the old working practices had got worse, and that intervention to prevent them had become even more troublesome. Instead of enhancing management prerogative, the new working arrangements were undermining it still further.

As working relationships deteriorated, management once again blamed the union for restricting co-operation on the shop floor, describing the shop stewards as 'devious' and 'unhelpful'. And the union drew upon the deep mistrust felt by workers effectively to prevent management from exercising control. The situation had changed little from the state of affairs which had existed prior to the introduction of the new working practices.

The resurrection of traditional views

Workers' reactions to the new working practices were plainly different in the two departments of the factory. In the vegetable department, relations between workers and supervisors never reached the fever pitch of adversarialism that characterised industrial relations in the meat department. But beyond this, the experience of both groups of workers shows that the new working arrangements did little to change workers' traditional perception of their own and management's interests. In each department managers, workers and shop stewards alike, interpreted developments within the factory in accordance with their traditional outlook.

Vegetable workers

The vegetable workers' unreformed attitudes towards management and union were further illustrated by their behaviour in a dispute over pay differentials. They had never felt closely involved with the union, believing that it operated largely for the benefit of the meat workers. Their sense of exclusion was heightened when they discovered that their colleagues in meat production had secured, for themselves alone through the union, an advantage in pay of about five pounds a week. Angry with the way they had been 'left out' they elected a new shop steward, an enthusiastic spokesman for their parity claim. After a good deal of unsuccessful remonstrating with management and the site convenor, the new steward and the vegetable workers took matters into their own hands. They banned overtime and in doing so threatened a considerable reduction in output.

Management decided to be 'decisive in conflict', even although they admitted in private that there was no sound justification for the differential between the two departments, and that the dispute was entirely the consequence of their earlier concession to the meat workers. When the vegetable workers did not show up for overtime on Sunday night, in accordance with 'Work or want', they were locked out on the following Monday morning. The convenor refused to support them and instead told them that they were 'out of procedure' and liable to be dismissed. A few days later they went back to work, their outburst of militancy having ended in defeat. The shop steward, elected to secure 'justice' on a popular issue, a 'cowboy' in the terminology of Batstone et al. (1977) resigned, believing that the union was not interested in his members. His stewardship was passed, uncontested, to a man well-liked by his colleagues, but seen as a 'clown' rather than a representative of sound judgement.

The dispute arose not just because management was weak in granting a concession to some workers and not others, but also because the vegetable workers were not closely involved in the activities of the local union. Their shop steward was relatively isolated from the other meat department stewards, and unskilled in developing the 'bargaining awareness' that suffused relations with management elsewhere in the factory. The popular election of a new shop steward did little to remedy this for he too was entirely inexperienced and at odds with his fellow representatives.

After the dispute, the workers in the vegetable department were further inclined to make their demands by themselves rather than relying on the union. Although they were unhappy about management's attempts to tighten-up, they preferred to raise issues directly at the consultative meetings, bypassing channels of union representation (and further contributing to their marginality in union decision-making). They knew that the supervisors were worried about their future, and decided to use it as an opportune lever. Although they were unable to find good arguments with which to defend their 'short-cut' ways of working, when the supervisors were too heavy handed in making interventions workers let them know of their views. During a consultative meeting, in complaining about supervisors spending too much time on the shop floor,

one of the men asked the supervisors if they were all competing for each other's jobs – the supervisors went berserk! (Worker)

They further exploited the supervisors' fears, by making use of their 'clown'. One afternoon, the supervisors became very agitated when they heard that their manager had received a complaint about them 'interfering' in the new working practices. The shop steward had gone straight to their superior without speaking to them first. In the words of one of the supervisors,

I got a phone call from the manager last night before the shift. The steward had been to see him because some of his members were claiming that supervisors were interfering. The steward had been to a stewards' meeting that afternoon, and the convenor told him that if it happened again he should organise a walk out. The steward went to see the manager, told him all this, and the manager rang me worried about it. He said we should try to find out who had complained, so we went down on the shop floor and asked them what the trouble was. The steward was there himself, and everybody turned round and said everything was fine. (Supervisor)

The shop steward, in his own words, had been 'set up and made to feel like a right patsy', by his members. They exploited the supervisors' insecurity at the expense of the union, for which they had little serious regard or loyalty.

In these ways, workers made clear to their supervisors that if they tried to use their authority too directly, they would suffer considerable embarrassment. Supervisors knew they couldn't press too hard for change. The vegetable workers played upon aspects of management politics to make a defence of 'short-cuts' which they found difficult to explicitly justify. When they found it hard to defend spending 'too much' time in the canteen their tactics were instead to rouse supervisors' fear of 'rocking the boat' and potential embarrassment should they try to put a stop to it. For some time, even although these ploys did not prevent supervisors eventually imposing greater control over workers, they were successful to a degree in holding up and softening management's attempt to claw back 'bad habits'. But equally, however, this behaviour reflected little more than opportunism, the use of sharp practice rather than tactics, because the insecurity of supervisors was a matter entirely in the hands of management. Vegetable workers' ability to influence events was therefore restricted to the manipulation of 'covert' matters which could not become part of any specific bargaining claim. Their 'bargaining awareness' was not developed to the point where they could use the working practices agreement to argue a legitimate case against management. Consequently when their opportunism drove them to industrial action, their failure to fashion an argument which might persuade other workers in the factory to support them enabled management to inflict swift defeat.

In short, although the vegetable workers preferred many aspects of the new arrangements, there was little in their behaviour to suggest that they had revised their attitudes towards management and unions. The new working practices met with less resistance in the vegetable department because arguing with managers was 'too much hassle' and achieved little, rather than on account of a positive accord between workers and managers. When management became dissatisfied with workers' efforts, workers expressed their resentment by delaying supervisors' attempts to make them work harder through forms of 'covert politics'. Their ultimate acquiescence in an extension of management prerogative was, however, a reflection of a traditional view of management authority, in part founded upon their longstanding estrangement from the local union. As in the past, their isolation deprived them of both the resolve and the organisation to develop effective tactics for opposing management. They complied with management not out of enthusiasm for corporate goals, but because they did not have the wherewithal to resist.

Meat workers

In the meat department, management found that it was impossible to extend prerogative to the same degree. It commonly attributed this difficulty to the behaviour of the shop stewards. Such reasoning, however, was probably too narrow an explanation, and reflected managers' uncritical appraisal of their own behaviour. As far as one can judge, the company's policy of tough discipline and extensive local bargaining encouraged a shop floor belief that a strong union was both a necessary and a desirable feature of factory life.

Workers' experiences of 'Work or want' left a clear and detailed impression upon them of the way in which their interests differed from those of the company. A coercive management style provided opportunities for 'bargaining awareness' to develop, and the skills of the shop stewards lay in fashioning these opportunities to create considerable support on the shop floor. The key to their continued success was the development of the union into a distinct organisation which displayed a clear understanding about the environment in which it operated, explicit goals related to its environment, and an ability to plan for the future. These attributes of union organisation enabled the stewards to maintain and augment their centrality in the processes of workplace decision-making.

The stewards' awareness of their environment was founded upon the recognition that management's ability to exert prerogatives over workers varied according to shifting circumstances:

We're under no illusions. The management need the tons at the moment. They'll behave differently when they don't need them. At the moment we hold all the cards but it may change. The management would love to make changes to our agreement but they know they can't. It's the plant problems that have prevented them from taking us on this year. (Shop steward)

Within this environment the stewards conceived of themselves as bargaining agents whose function was to manipulate circumstances in their members' interests. Their role was to co-ordinate the pressures which workers could bring to bear against management. To this end, they frequently met and talked together to develop their tactics, taking advantage of management's desperate desire for more output in a variety of ways. For example, as part of a 'withdrawal of co-operation',

we went round telling people to speed up rotation, just so as we could add the little extra bit of pressure. (Shop steward)

The attitudes and behaviour of the shop stewards reflected their self-image not as plain delegates acting as a conduit for workers' demands but as leaders with their own political authority and resources. For example, during the dispute over 'bulk boxes' and 'extra duties' (in which management attempted to argue that workers were required to cover duties not mentioned in the new working practices agreement), the stewards activated 'an arrangement' with their fellow shop stewards in the cold store. The cold store workers controlled the flow of raw materials and finished products throughout the factory, and an alliance with them which resulted in the blacking of products which were in dispute soon forced management to give way. The development of powerful 'arrangements' was a consequence of leadership which was substantially independent of management. Like all political leaders, therefore, the stewards used their authority to make deals which enhanced their own credibility and effectiveness.

From their position of leadership, the shop stewards formed careful judgements about their opponents. They knew which managers could manage the adversarial process skilfully and which could not. The skilful managers had tactics and would make clever bargains. Singling out a particular manager, one of stewards said,

you've got to watch him. He's very clever and shrewd – he'll make you give something to get something and he *never* says he will do something unilaterally. (Shop steward)

It was hard for the stewards to deal with this manager because his skill in making informal deals could have unforeseen future consequences. Furthermore, it was more difficult to turn an intricate exchange of undertakings about the future into clear messages which they could carry back to members. But another manager, prone to issuing 'instructions' and threatening discipline almost straight away, provided them with a much clearer shop floor symbol of management's coercive intentions. His actions posed a clear threat around which they could build support for their position. It was this manager that provoked the dispute over 'extra duties'. Instead of negotiating change, his immediate recourse to 'Work or want' provided the stewards with an opportunity to prevent management establishing an undesirable custom. His 'over the top' attitude enabled them to mobilise members in support of strike action. In short, like skilled politicians the stewards didn't simply declare an immutable position: their tactics varied depending upon which manager they were dealing with. Those managers most committed to 'Work or want' made it easier for the stewards to foster support, and they quickly took advantage of their opponents' errors.

Beneath the hustle of continuous bargaining and the discussion of tactics, the stewards had formed a common ideological or philosophical view of their situation. They described their relationship with management in adversarial language, in terms of 'a game' in which their role was 'to keep the pressure up'. As one might expect in a view rooted in the idea of contest, the participants were ascribed clear objectives. For the stewards, the function of management was to extract continuously more effort from workers whilst offering the minimum in return, and their own role was to keep management constantly in check. The influence of their organisation, in the adversarial circumstances of the 'game', depended upon workers sticking to certain rules described by the stewards as 'basic union principles'. The 'principles' conferred an identity upon the union and gave meaning to its status as an organisation.

'Union principles' were not an outright rejection of the need for sustained and efficient production. The stewards often expressed their commitment to the future of the company and, just like management, they believed that the new working practices were an essential ingredient of success against competitor firms. Their values were not distilled from a broad view of politics but were largely a reaction to management behaviour. Although the stewards' authority rested in part upon their skilful manipulation of shop floor perceptions of management, their motivation was rooted in their own shop floor experience of the company's treatment of employees. In conversation, they disassociated themselves from 'militants' interested in securing wider political ends. They argued that in the past, when given an opportunity, management's traditional commitment to tough discipline had led it to behave in an 'excessive' or 'unreasonable' way. The union's role was therefore the legitimate and unceasing defence of worker interests. 'Union principles' were founded upon a sceptical view of management's competence and trustworthiness.

'Union principles' also provided a stable cultural foundation for the union, constituting an expression of faith in the twin virtues of collectivism and leadership. They were the lens through which the shop stewards viewed the potential and the problems inherent in the new working practices. At their heart was the view that workers' interests could be secured only if collectivism was directed and maintained by the stewards, and this in turn provided the stewards with clear, shared beliefs about their long term goals. The new working practices, in the stewards' view, embodied the potential for strengthened commitment to 'union principles'. The modus operandi of work groups should, therefore, combine improvements in efficiency with a collective outlook towards shop floor relations with management. Only in this way would it be possible to ensure that the new working practices delivered long term benefits to workers. It was for this reason that the arguments about job rotation acquired such enormous fervour. From the viewpoint of the shop floor, management intentions appeared not to support but instead to threaten a collective disposition towards work. The stewards, who saw their role as maintaining the resources of opposition necessary in dealings with management, made recourse to 'union principles' in order to support their argument. They sought to foster a powerful sense of shop floor collectivism:

Basic trades union principles come into play. They [the management] wanted to kick thirty people out of the building. We won't let them be kicked out. In the end we said take one out and you'll lose the lot. (Shop steward)

The stewards admitted that certain workers were finding the wider range of tasks too demanding. But they strongly suspected that management was trying to dispense with workers it deemed unproductive and formed a clear judgement of the situation. From the union's point of view, the solution to the problem was a matter for the work groups themselves:

Where you've got a guy that can't manage all the jobs, the group can make allowances and work round him. They should carry him. (Convenor)

The union informally discouraged work groups from thinking that they might expel workers they didn't want to 'carry' because such actions were antithetical to 'union principles':

You can't have the guys falling out with each other, saying, 'I don't want to work with him', and 'he's no good let's get rid of him and get somebody else'. The management would love that. (Convenor)

The stewards had become equally well aware that management was trying to reduce their position as purveyors of shop floor opinion, and they were similarly determined to prevent this. In these circumstances the stewards' objective was to prevent their position as leaders from being undermined. They made regular rounds of the shop floor, checking on supervisors' behaviour, ensuring that work groups were not persuaded to agree to changes without due negotiation taking place. They insisted on being present at all the weekly consultative meetings to make sure that managers did not use them to alter working practices. During one meeting, the manager suggested that following damage to a machine during cleaning, the operator should in future be supervised by a fitter. The steward quickly stopped him. It was, in his view, 'a negotiating issue' and the manager didn't persist. In this instance, as in others, the stewards prevailed in the role of worker representative at the expense of management prerogative. Such an approach enabled them to retain their influence over matters of work organisation.

The power of tradition

Traditional characteristics of shop floor behaviour in both departments of the factory continued as before, unaltered by the introduction of the new working arrangements. Workers were no more inclined to accept the authority of management, nor did their views on the trades union change much. In the vegetable department, workers expressed resentment at management's attempts to make them work harder, but ultimately their acquiescence reflected their views that managerial prerogative had, in essence, changed very little. As before, they continued to believe that the trades union had little to offer them and continued to remain distant from the activities of the shop stewards elsewhere in the factory. In the meat department, the activities of the well organised shop stewards continued as before. 'Basic union principles' continued to be enormously influential at the expense of management as, contrary to management expectations, the new method of organising work provided a horde of opportunities for developing custom and practice. In both areas of the factory, workers continued to feel that their interests differed from management, and the way they expressed this view remained unchanged. Traditions persisted.

For this reason the way in which the factory was run changed far less than the company intended. From the company's point of view, the purpose of the new working practices was partly to restore the influence of line management over production, eliminating union 'interference' and, by implication, reducing the importance of the personnel department in production matters. However, as things turned out, the factory personnel manager and the union convenor, who had both been enormously important in the past, successfully maintained power over their respective constituents, and once again made themselves seem 'indispensable' in preventing co-operation breaking down completely. Both individuals expressed continued mutual commitment to their 'good working relationship'. It came into play, for example, on the thorny issue of job rotation.

The personnel manager slipped 'inside information' to the convenor, telling him of the mounting evidence to suggest that the newly installed machinery was an important cause of production difficulties. He explained that line management found itself unable to admit that such expensive new machinery could be unsuitable and they preferred instead to pin most of the blame on inefficient working practices. On this basis, the personnel manager persuaded the convenor that if workers reduced the speed of rotation and production still remained below target, line management would have to think again about what was causing the problems. It was undoubtedly the case that making such an admission to the workforce would have been a heavy blow to line managers' feelings of competence and professionalism. Their claim to technical competence, was after all, an essential part of the moral authority supporting their right to manage production. But by providing the convenor with this insight, and by securing his agreement to reduce the rate of job rotation, the personnel manager tacitly enlisted his support in a tricky matter of management politics. The convenor exercised considerable authority over the stewards. He was respected for his insights and his shrewdness and the stewards, who were convinced that their own effectiveness depended upon their exercising leadership, were similarly prepared to accept, in principle, the leadership of the convenor. When he made a decision they were inclined after some argument, to accept it:

There was a discussion amongst the stewards and the convenor for quite a few hours. It was very heated. At first we [the stewards] told him [the convenor] that he wasn't on. We said, 'if we've got to go down the road then we'll go down the road'. That's where we left it one day. Then the next day the convenor called us back and told us straight. As the senior steward, with the negotiating committee behind him, we should give the slower rotation a try. He told us that it would show the management that it was the machines that were the problem, not the men. Looking back I can see he was right. (Shop steward)

The convenor's instruction put the shop stewards in an embarrassing position. Asking their constituents to comply with management's request was not easy, because there was some considerable enthusiasm for industrial action. But the stewards asked the members nevertheless because their commitment to 'union principles' outweighed the immediate pressures put upon them by the shop floor. At a time in which line management 'excuses' for poor production centred upon the 'idle' and 'insolent' behaviour of workers, the relationship between the personnel manager and the convenor provided an opportunity to change line managers' view of the situation, without resort to conflict that would have been costly for both parties.

The relationship between the convenor and the personnel manager not only helped the personnel manager to win arguments against line managers, it also helped the union to win arguments against line management too. For example, in the 'bulk box' dispute the personnel manager was instrumental in persuading line management to concede that extra labour should be provided, thereby averting the near certainty of a 24 hour stoppage. In short, the strength of this informal relationship between the convenor and the personnel manager reinforced both the power of the union leadership and sustained the influence of personnel management *vis-à-vis* line management. It perpetuated the influence of both during the introduction of new working practices which otherwise threatened their positions. And it ensured that the way in which the factory was managed was not significantly changed.

Two years later

Some time after fieldwork was completed, the works personnel manager retired and several other managers moved on to jobs elsewhere. It seems that in the absence of the 'good working relationship' between the convenor and the local personnel manager, industrial relations deteriorated further. The new management team decided to regain control of the situation. They presented the union with a familiar catalogue of bad working practices, including excessive break periods, bad shift changes and persistent lateness. The union felt under pressure to make concessions and, according to the convenor, 'acted to clear out the abuse'. But the management then brought further pressure to bear by raising discussion of alleged incidents in which shop stewards had been deliberately obstructive, for example, by refusing to allow 'minor' changes to production schedules without the provision of extra staff. In these ways, management sought higher standards of discipline, and it began to challenge the position of individual shop stewards.

In private, management planned more radical alterations to shop floor life. It drew up plans to reduce the number of workers on production lines and, more importantly, renewed its intention to eliminate the influence of the union from routine changes in production. As in the past, its objective was to secure management's right to decide how many staff should be deployed, and it proposed to restrict the exercise of the union's right of appeal to the end of a trial period lasting several months.

Management sanctioned considerable overtime and stockpiled enough product to last several weeks. Then it sent its suggestions to the union. One afternoon whilst the shop stewards were out of the department (attending a meeting in the convenor's office to discuss the proposals), managers unilaterally implemented them on the shop floor. As far as one can judge, it seems clear that the company wanted to provoke a strike for it believed there was no other way to break the shop floor power of the stewards.

A ballot was hastily arranged and there was a substantial majority in favour of an indefinite stoppage. A series of conciliation meetings ended in failure. In the third week of the strike, with little prospect of achieving a settlement, the management threatened to sue the union for damages. An oversight on the part of the union's full time officers meant that the ballot papers had not fully complied with modern legal requirements. This mistake necessitated a further ballot in which there was a narrow majority in favour of a return to work. In the following weeks some of the shop stewards, including the convenor, opted for voluntary redundancy.

Conclusions

Management introduced the new working practices to improve productivity and to remove barriers to efficient working. Its thinking about the future was an eclectic mixture of forward thinking and past experience. On the one hand, it sought to improve productivity by providing workers with more fulfilling jobs, on the other it remained firmly committed to its tough, traditional approach to discipline.

Implementing the new approach to industrial relations was difficult. The company's attempts to establish new standards of effort by making unsuitable workers redundant ended in defeat at the hands of the well organised union. Under the leadership of capable shop stewards, the threat of unemployment strengthened (rather than weakened) workers' resolve to maintain the principle of 'last in first out'. Consequently those workers introduced to the new working practices were those with the greatest experience of past industrial relations. Attempts to fashion a more unitarist style of decision-making also ran into difficulties because management was obliged to involve the shop stewards in the design of the new working practices. Despite extensive discussions and detailed agreements, management and unions had little clear understanding of their rights and obligations towards each other.

Workers undoubtedly preferred many aspects of the new working practices, in part because they had greater variety and discretion in their jobs, and also because they were afforded greater opportunities for leisure. They valued these opportunities above extra effort to the benefit of the company. In the leeway provided by autonomous working, numerous 'short-cuts' emerged. In the vegetable department supervisors managed to restrain some of them. Their success was in part because these workers were more inclined to accept a view of extensive management prerogative that was deeply rooted in their work experience prior to the new practices. But it was also due to their estrangement from the tradition of strong union organisation in the plant. Without union organisation they could not develop sustainable arguments to use against management. In the meat department management attempts to influence working practices failed. Disputes arose over poor production figures. Management doubted the willingness and competence of workers; workers doubted the intentions of management. In an environment of deepening mistrust management could not command moral authority to manage and the shop stewards were able to re-establish their influence over work. The nature of their union organisation drew its strength from management's preference for tough discipline.

What is most striking in these developments is the way in which traditional behaviour re-established itself so quickly within the new working practices. Amongst previously well organised groups of workers, traditional suspicion of management re-asserted itself to prevent an extension of managerial prerogative. Where there were uncertainties in the production process, for example those associated with the operation of new machinery, a good deal of co-operation was needed. But low trust turned an opportunity for co-operation into stoutly defended custom and practice. Co-operation became so limited that management escalated conflict by provoking a strike to break the power of the stewards, it hoped, once and for all.

Management succeeded in winning the strike, and in reducing the number of production workers required. But the real reason for its labour relations difficulties was not as it believed, unco-operative shop stewards, but its own policy of 'Work or want' which contributed so much to the development of 'union principles'. 'Work or want' was instrumental in reinforcing the division of interests between managers and workers, cultivating at best low commitment to management goals, and at worst an adversarial climate in which it was difficult for either side to make progress towards a better understanding of the other. Management's tendency to set aside moral persuasion and resort to coercion proved a major impediment to change. Following the strike, its achievement was the subordination of workers, rather than progress towards genuine and extensive co-operation at work.

Chapter 4 turns away from attempts to implement a unitarist reform of work on the shop floor, and instead examines the case of a workplace where management, decidedly old-fashioned in many respects, paid continuous and careful attention to building a climate of shop floor co-operation through explicit recognition of a diversity of interests. Might it be the case that the skilful management of pluralism can succeed in generating co-operation and flexibility without need for conflict and confrontation?

4   The biscuit works

Introduction

Companies which have publicised their 'new industrial relations' have often captured a good deal of attention in recent years. Enthusiastic accounts of new developments have often portrayed previous methods of working as old-fashioned and uncompetitive. Some advocates of the 'new industrial relations' have implied that the spread of new approaches will be inevitable and universal on account of their potential for improved efficiency, achieved both through a reduction in supervisory overheads and the liberation of workers' individual talents. Yet in the search for something new, commentators have perhaps been too ready to set aside the lessons and ideas of the past. The biscuit works which is the subject of this chapter provides an opportunity to examine the extent and means by which a decidedly orthodox approach to industrial relations can be reconciled with modern competitive pressures.

One might suppose that even in corporations where high levels of trust have been established for many years, changing external circumstances have placed harmful stress upon long-established relationships and practices (Fox 1974 p.307). For this reason it is interesting to examine what degree of co-operation is nowadays sustainable within traditional approaches. As many companies have increasingly preferred to appeal to workers directly, without the involvement of trades unions, the biscuit works provides an opportunity to review whether consultation with worker representatives and careful adherence to formal agreements can bring forth the co-operation and flexibility necessary for competitive production.

This chapter illustrates how, twenty years ago, senior management at the biscuit company came to the view that a joint approach to industrial relations offered the best prospect for developing a climate of co-operation at work. It shows how this was achieved, and examines the way in which the 'joint approach' is presently working upon the shop floor. The role of managers, shop stewards and workers in contemporary shop floor life is explored. During the 1980s the company rationalised production, closed several factories, and progressively modernised those which remained open. By and large, a substantial reorganisation of production was introduced without significant alterations to management style. Instead, the company continued with its existing policies for managing shop floor industrial relations, an approach which had in the past successfully secured both stability and co-operation. The introduction of change required that managers and workers assimilate new developments within the existing terms of their relations, rather than refashioning them entirely along new lines. The way in which the biscuit company reconciled competitive pressures with goodwill on the shop floor over the past twenty years can be explained through a process of continuous adaptation. This study suggests that by devising institutional mechanisms to inhibit adversarial behaviour, and the continuous maintenance of a shop floor culture of flexibility and co-operation, there may be more than one way for managers to achieve high levels of worker motivation and flexibility.

The biscuit works was one amongst several owned by a successful multinational company which was formed through the amalgamation of a number of independent producers. The company held a considerable slice of the market for biscuits and cakes in conjunction with other large producers with whom it competed hard for orders from powerful supermarket chains. Although the company produced both a mixture of unbranded products (which supermarkets sold under their own label) and quality 'branded' lines, the biscuit works studied here specialised in producing the latter in very high volumes. The plant was mature, having been established for over fifty years. It was also large both in comparison with others within the company and by the standards of the plants owned by the company's competitors. About 1,000 people were employed at the works, a figure which had declined slowly through natural wastage and voluntary redundancy from a peak of about 1,700 reached during the early 1970s. The decline in employment was caused by the gradual introduction of automated machinery on some production lines, and by all accounts the plant was technically complex by the standards present elsewhere in the industry. Still, however, the production of biscuits involved a good deal of manual labour, mostly drawn from the surrounding district. The shop floor comprised a high proportion of first and second generation immigrants, a polyglot community including Asians, West Indians and Eastern Europeans.

The company recognised several unions and a powerful corporate personnel department conducted pay negotiations and job evaluation at company level with plant convenors and full time union officers. Well established and agreed company-wide procedures for handling discipline, grievances and disputes were also in place. At the plant, there were two personnel managers, a trainee personnel manager, and a personnel officer, who were involved in local discussions on staffing and disciplinary matters. Several unions were recognised at the site. This study focuses mainly upon the activities of unskilled and semi-skilled manual workers, nearly all of whom were in the recognised manual union, and a small number of supervisors, most of whom were in an affiliated union. There were around a dozen shop stewards representing shop floor unskilled manuals and chargehands, and a full time manual convenor for whom the company provided an office on site and various secretarial facilities. The formal institutional arrangements for managing industrial relations at the biscuit works therefore bore a striking resemblance to those in place at the frozen food works, being typical of those present in large and mature manufacturing establishments.

Twenty years before: from unitarism to pluralism

The challenges of competition are not new. Towards the end of the 1960s the biscuit company made a substantial reorganisation of its production facilities. At this time it did not recognise trades unions in any of its plants. But senior managers believed that their plan to close nearly half the company's factories and to concentrate production through expansion of a few remaining ones might result in industrial disruption if trades unions made use of the opportunity to recruit members.

Taking the view that unilateral decision-making was no longer appropriate to the late 1960s, management's policy on labour relations underwent a sea-change. It planned the introduction of carefully controlled joint regulation of work. The executive responsible for the changes explained some years afterwards,

my advice was that without a plan we would end up in a most terrible situation, perhaps getting unions we didn't want. I advocated that we speak to the unions in confidence ... and invite those unions we wanted to recruit in our factories. (Senior executive)

Since the purpose of union recognition was to encourage the formation of a credible workers' representative body for purposes of collective bargaining, management intended to encourage workers to become union members and decided upon a policy of automatically deducting union dues from their wages. Equally, however, it knew that widespread local bargaining would be time-consuming and difficult to control and instead favoured company-wide rather than plant negotiations. By eliminating the scope for inconsistencies to arise locally, it believed it had narrowed opportunities for the growth of unhelpful custom and practice.

Other authors have found examples of the way in which management attitudes towards unions changed around this time. Terry (1979) suggested that during the 1970s management may have often encouraged and shaped the development of trade union organisation in previously non-union workplaces. Nichols and Beynon (1977) illustrated how sophisticated managements can exert a powerful influence over the attitudes of union members in order to create a climate of opinion highly favourable to management goals. In their account the union retained the appearance of independence, but was unable to function in ways which were against management interests.

It is perhaps worth remembering, however, that the decision to recognise and support the development of trades unions cannot have been easy for managers to accept. Whatever the measure of support given to trades unions by the Donovan Commission (1968), in many circumstances, managements' decision was more a reflection of pragmatism than of conviction (Spencer 1985 p.24). This was true in part at the biscuit works, where managers were already having difficulty making traditional unilateral regulation work. The leading union activist of the time, later to become convenor, recalled,

the job grading scheme was made up by the factory director – he did all the jobs and made all the decisions. Jobs were graded one to four, but in order to get the proper grade your performance had to be satisfactory. This was decided by your chargehand and your manager. It led to blue eyed boys and victimisation. You could be doing a grade one job but only getting grade three pay. Managers were knocking off some of the women and in return putting them in the better jobs. Then there were bleeders like the manager who made sure people didn't get their Christmas bonus. He didn't mind them sneaking off to the toilets for a smoke during the year but come Christmas he would discipline them. (Convenor 1969–85)

Furthermore, senior management's decision to recognise trades unions met with resistance from local managers who resented their authority being challenged and did not share their superiors' view of a pluralist future:

I managed to get every man in the department into the union. Half of the women joined too. We got up to around 350 members in three months. Then the managers clamped down. They started to make my life a misery. Sometimes they would say somebody had claimed I was harassing them. Or whatever I managed to get for somebody they would withdraw it. Then they said we couldn't collect money [union subscriptions]. As a result we started to lose membership, so it got to the situation where I said, 'Hell if we're going to lose membership then we may as well go out with a bang'. I decided to call the factory out on strike! (Convenor 1969–85)

The leader of the local union set about finding good reason for a stoppage. He hit upon insisting that union members could not work alongside non-union workers, and added a pay demand for good measure. When, as predicted, local management refused to concede these demands, the union members walked out. The company chairman was worried about the consequences but the senior management stuck clearly to their company-wide aims and set about defeating the militants on the shop floor:

We [senior management] forced a meeting with the chairman, and forced him, against his will, to let the strike continue. After two weeks the local union was on its knees. I threatened the national officers that I would tear up the [proposed recognition] agreement. (Senior executive)

The union withdrew support for the local strikers, the strike collapsed a few days later, and a formal recognition agreement was signed shortly afterwards. The company, whatever it might have threatened, preferred not to tear up the recognition proposal. And the local union activists gained only a highly centralised set of negotiating arrangements, in which national union officers played a dominant role.

Senior management had developed a clear policy for managing industrial relations. It calculated that recognition of trades unions offered opportunities for promoting co-operation and stability in industrial relations. By involving the union in the company's plans for change, management believed that it could add legitimacy to its decisions at little expense to its prerogative (Fox 1974 p.302). Taking the view that a unilateral style of decision-making could no longer inspire workers to full acceptance of management, the company established procedures for joint regulation of future terms and conditions, the purpose of which was to contain conflict and promote a spirit of management by agreement.

To further strengthen its authority in fashioning company-wide bargains, management placed individual factories in competition with each other. The production of the company's major brands was distributed between works to ensure that no single plant could bring production of a major brand to a complete halt. These arrangements served as both a precaution and a disincentive to local industrial action by reducing the power of strategic groups of workers (Purcell 1983 p.59). Furthermore, despite the current advocacy for dealing with as few trades unions as possible, the company decided to offer the right to represent shop floor workers to different trades unions at different plants:

I follow my great predecessors in these things: divide and conquer! If you have two unions representing the same sort of workers it's far better than having one. (Senior executive)

During the 1980s these arrangements were effective in creating an element of rivalry between plants which worked wholly to management's advantage. As a further round of plant closures was enacted, workers did little to offer support to their colleagues facing impending redundancy:

When the company shut the other factories, the reaction here was, 'Oh good. Thank God it's not us'. (Line manager)

Attempts to foster some measure of union solidarity between plants had never come to much. The works convenor tried, on several occasions, to arrange meetings with convenors from other factories but few showed up. On another occasion he refused to accept the transfer of a product from another factory:

I said 'Hell, No! We can't take the bread out of their mouths'. The next thing I hear is that those bastards up North have taken it. Much good that it did them. They've shut them down as well now! (Convenor 1969–85)

The interests of each factory were divided and union goals at each plant were opportunist.

The company's adherence to national bargaining over all major aspects of terms and conditions exercised a powerful effect upon the local union's attitude towards change. Tied down by national negotiations it adopted an accommodating position:

Ours was the most modern factory. I don't know why. Accident I think at first, but then by design. The management wanted to introduce new machinery. I was faced with a dilemma. Should I let it in or not? I thought about it and said, 'O.K fine!', I couldn't see the point of trying to save jobs when there was still full employment. (Convenor 1969–85)

Co-operating with the introduction of new machinery ensured that the factory remained in a favoured position relative to others in the company. At the same time it offered modest scope for enhancing wages because management reckoned that jobs attached to new machinery were more technically demanding and offered higher rates of pay for them. But even a policy of prudent accommodation offered the local union few bargaining opportunities. New jobs were graded by a manager and a shop steward from another plant visiting the factory to act as 'independent' assessors. Although the local union could submit a request for a re-examination of job grades it had no influence upon the result. The convenor continued the policy of submitting requests for regrading, but he knew it offered him little leverage.

In a regrading job grades can go down as well as up. (Convenor 1985 onwards)

By creating an element of competition between the plants, and by conducting negotiations well away from the shop floor, management was largely successful in inhibiting bargaining opportunities for local shop stewards.

Management was not always able to use these tactics without difficulty, however. During the late 1970s peaceful relations had been seriously threatened by a small group of 'hard-line' shop stewards. They organised a series of walk-outs and attempted to depose the convenor. Activists levelled the accusation, supported by a disconcerting number of workers, that the 'union establishment' was 'in the pocket of the company' and a significant management concession was necessary to save the situation. To keep control, the convenor sought an issue on which to consolidate his support amongst the workforce. He demanded that the company pay workers during meal breaks and threatened an overtime ban. Anxious to prevent either industrial action or the hard-line faction winning control of the local union, the works manager conceded the demand almost immediately. Payment for meal breaks was dressed up in such a way as to appear to managers elsewhere in the company that it was the result of productivity improvement. But the reality, understood on the shop floor, was that the deal was simply payment for practices which had long been part of normal working. The convenor gained considerable acclaim from the workforce. The paid meal break was popularly regarded as his personal achievement and the challenge from the hard-line stewards collapsed. Although the company could not directly influence who became elected shop stewards, it had, on the whole, developed a climate of industrial relations which was highly favourable to efficient production. It had also successfully prevented the local union from developing bargaining opportunities.

This chapter examines how management's bold 1960s initiative fared on the shop floor in more recent times, following another period of substantial company reorganisation. To what extent were local managers able to incorporate trades unions within their decision-making? Were the shop stewards, who were inexperienced and easy to deal with at the outset, still amenable to management overtures? Or did their experiences in the course of representing workers' interests limit their sympathies with management initiatives and encourage them, as many commentators have thought likely, in more independent and assertive behaviour (Batstone 1984 p.257; Harris 1987)? Answers to these questions are important in assessing how the firm coped with the contemporary challenge of competition.

The present day shop floor

The large scale production of biscuits involves several distinct tasks, namely, preparing dough, stretching and cutting it to the right shape, baking the dough to produce biscuits, and finally wrapping the finished biscuits in packets and transport cases. There were ten production lines in the part of the works included in this study, employing a total of about 250 unskilled and semi-skilled manual workers. Each one was situated adjacent to the next, and staffed by teams of process workers and packing workers. For the most part workers were employed on a particular line although there was some exchange of staff, skills permitting, within and between lines to cover for absences, sickness and holidays.

The men who mixed dough worked in a small group, loading powdered ingredients into machines which were otherwise entirely automatic. The dough was then fed directly to cutting machines, tended by machine drivers whose responsibility was to ensure that biscuit shapes conformed to precise dimensions through making fine running adjustments to their machinery. Oven operators controlled the temperature in various stages of the long continuously fed ovens. Just like the machine drivers, the oven operators were required to make periodic adjustments to the ovens, exercising discretion and judgement in the process. By doing so they controlled the texture and colour of the biscuits. There was generally one machine driver and one oven operator working on each production line. From the ovens the biscuits were transported on long conveyor belts to each of the packing lines. A machine collected the biscuits prior to their being fed into the wrapping machines. Two workers ensured the uninterrupted supply of biscuits to the wrapping machine by performing a series of minor tasks such as removing broken biscuits. A third operator worked the wrapping machine, changing the packaging film periodically and clearing machine jams. A fourth inspected the packet end seals, and finally a team of workers packed the biscuits into cases ready to be transported to the warehouse. Packing workers generally rotated around packing tasks on a daily basis. Some of the production lines had rather more sophisticated machinery in which the final packing was automated.

Round the clock operations were maintained in 'the process' (mixing, cutting, and baking) by two 8 hour shifts which were extended by regular 'structured overtime' shared between workers. On the packaging lines, two 8 hour shifts were supplemented by a mixture of structured overtime and an evening shift of part time workers. Most full time workers were accustomed to working large amounts of overtime as a means of boosting their earnings. The packing lines were generally staffed by women during the day and (short) evening shifts, and by men during the night shift.

Managers

Management exercised very close control over work through a complex hierarchy of supervisors and managers. Every aspect of work was closely supervised. Workers in the 'process' reported directly to a foreman. He had the formal responsibility of allocating their overtime hours and tasks. In the packing hall, the packing teams were under the direct supervision of chargehands working on each of the packing lines. Amongst other things, they were responsible for recording the late arrival of workers, and were formally in charge of allocating workers to particular jobs. Their responsibility was to ensure that workers kept the lines running efficiently by encouraging them to free machine jams quickly and by acting speedily to prevent products from being wasted in the event of mechanical problems. Above the foremen and supervisors were a number of managers each with responsibility for two lines, a further tier of management, and finally the departmental manager himself. Even the most senior grades of management visited the production lines frequently, examining work and talking to the machine operators.

In the twenty years since unions had been recognised, management had come to involve the union in determining detailed features of the work routine, making it an integral part of the rule-making process. For example, it involved the shop stewards in resolving a spate of squabbles which broke out on the packing lines over instances of favouritism shown by the chargehands towards particular workers. Workers alleged that chargehands sometimes avoided marking their 'favourites' as late, or would reserve the best jobs on their line for workers that they liked best. For an outsider these disputes might seem petty, but for those involved the distribution of good and bad jobs raised issues of 'justice' and 'fairness' which had great bearing upon the quality of working life:

If you go to another line the chargehands will take their girls off packing and make you pack instead. If you say anything you get labelled as a trouble-maker. (Worker)

Line managers resolved these difficulties in characteristic fashion. For example,

once when I was late because of the train, the chargehand said, 'I've saved this job for you', but it wasn't my job that day anyway. I said 'no'. I got the manager and the shop steward and we went in the office and now it doesn't happen any more ... The managers don't show favouritism. They're fair. (Worker)

In this instance, the manager and the shop steward made an agreement that in future, if a worker was more than 15 minutes late their job would be reallocated and they would fill the place of an absentee on another line. Managers' willingness to enter into detailed agreements with the union on such matters was a measure of the extent to which joint decision-making had entered into the culture of the works. Managers recognised that such arrangements caused little inconvenience, posed little threat to prerogative, and provided a reliable means of alleviating the frictions which impaired workers' motivation. Moreover they recognised that their willingness to make agreements in the interests of 'fairness' did much to improve morale, cultivating their own esteem and the reputation of the shop stewards in the workers' estimation.

Line managers generally involved shop stewards to a similar degree in decisions about discipline. Although they did not discipline workers very often, on the few occasions when they did they knew the importance of following joint procedures carefully. On previous occasions when some of them had acted 'out of procedure' their recommendations had been overturned by their superiors. Both line managers and workers told stories about managers who had been obliged to provide written apologies for unreasonable behaviour towards individuals. In fact, senior management not only insisted that junior management adhere to the written procedure, it also provided incentives for shop stewards to do the same. It had long adopted the custom of reducing by one degree on appeal whatever disciplinary penalty a junior manager imposed. The convention made management appear all the more reasonable and able to take a sympathetic view of workers' circumstances. By the same token, this convention also made shop stewards appear effective advocates for their members.

Matters did not always proceed this smoothly. For example, on one occasion a nightshift shop steward refused to co-operate with the procedure when managers tried to discipline an oven operator for burning biscuits. He 'stormed out' of the disciplinary meeting arguing that management had made no case. Managers speculated that the shop steward concerned was trying to look assertive shortly before his office became due for election. But whatever was the truth of the matter, his refusal to conform prevented management from reducing the worker's penalty on appeal and, by normal standards, the worker concerned received rather too severe a punishment. Later the departmental manager and the personnel officer spoke severely to the factory convenor. They reminded him of his responsibilities to ensure that procedures were adhered to by shop stewards. The convenor in turn spoke to the steward, threatening to take away his union card. Faced with the possibility of isolation, the recalcitrant steward agreed to abide by the rules in future. In these ways management was committed to creating an environment in which discipline was seen to be fair because it was handled jointly. It sought actively to involve the union in the processes of discipline and bolster the apparent effectiveness of its role.

In the twenty years since recognition, managers had therefore come to accept that the union could be an integral part of the way in which the works was managed. But not only was the union an important part of current routines, it was integral to the company's plans progressively to modernise the factory. Management carefully encouraged active union participation in discussions over the introduction of new equipment and associated reductions in staff levels. Shop stewards were always informed of changes to be made to the lines, whereupon line managers and shop stewards would agree a revised number of staff and there would be a trial, lasting several days. Both managers and stewards observed the line at intervals throughout the trial, and then met once again to discuss adjustments to their initial plans.

To the shop floor, this highly visible procedure conveyed an impression of joint regulation. But managers looked upon the negotiations primarily as a act of theatre. Although they deliberately prolonged the process to make outcomes look as if they were the result of a vigorous contest, managers felt themselves to be comfortably in charge of discussions. One of them recounted recent discussions on a line as follows:

Months before the new wrapping machine arrived we started negotiating. The union said 12 people. So I said 6. There was uproar but I wouldn't budge off 6. Then I started to bully them a bit. They suggested 11 and I increased my offer to 7. So we had a 'failure to agree' and it went up to the next level of management. By now they had come down to 9. We agreed to 9 as long as they agreed to operate another new machine when it arrived. Logic isn't the answer in these situations. I try to find a way of making sure they don't lose face and I allow them to negotiate me up. (Line manager)

Another manager described how the introduction of a new generation of highly automated packing lines was stage-managed with similar expertise:

We invited the shop stewards from each shift to come and observe the line over a three or four week period. We had a lot of teething troubles but we kept running it with three people. [After the trial] the union wanted five and after a number of adjournments they suggested four. We reconvened the next day and I made out that four was a major concession. They didn't know I had set the cost standard as four in the first place! (Senior manager)

Managers believed there was no benefit in negotiating with the shop stewards if the stewards always felt beaten afterwards. Sometimes they allowed the shop stewards easy and complete victories in instances where the company's long term interests were not threatened. For example, prior to temporary alterations to a particular line, management conceded a union demand for more labour than it had initially intended:

If this had been a long run set up we would have stuck it out ... but there was no point in arguing for just four or five weeks. (Line manager)

It was not always possible to manipulate the shop stewards in negotiations. On occasions the nightshift shop stewards stubbornly refused to give in to pressure and caused management a good deal of irritation. A senior manager was of the clear view that a steward was being deliberately obstructive for personal ends:

He [one of the nightshift shop stewards] is after one thing – redundancy. I've told him that if there's any redundancy going I'll personally make sure that he's the last one on the list. (Senior manager)

Sometimes when shop stewards became unco-operative managers would take a rather tougher line. It had long been the custom that when the lines were running smoothly, dayshift workers on overtime finished 45 minutes early, leaving their machines to be tended by a handful of nightshift men. The nightshift men clocked out their colleagues at the appointed finishing time. Although this practice was against the rules, managers were happy to turn a blind eye. Such co-operation between workers had little detrimental effect upon production and was generally accepted by management as a legitimate means of circumventing the rigidities of clocking (Arthurs and Kinnie 1984 p.24). But when one of the nightshift shop stewards argued that the dayshift practice of leaving early should also be permissible for nightshift workers on dayshift overtime, on the grounds that management had already accepted the principle of leaving early, he was firmly rebuffed. Management refused his request arguing that the situation was getting out of hand. Moreover it deftly turned the argument back on the steward and 'in the interests of fairness', it disallowed the practice amongst dayshift workers too! In part, the shop steward's lack of success might be attributed to his lack of bargaining skill. But management, already unhappy about the way in which this informal practice was developing (see below) used the opportunity to teach the steward a lesson. They had become fed up with his cavalier attitude towards formal procedure and were determined to curtail his attempts to expand informal practices. His fruitless attempt to win popularity with his constituents backfired conspicuously, and also worked at the expense of workers on other shifts. It caused the steward considerable embarrassment in the period immediately prior to his election.

On the whole, however, management did not face sustained or co-ordinated opposition. The common feature of management and union encounters was the way in which management provided a role for the union to play, and generally encouraged the belief on the shop floor that the shop stewards had independently secured concessions. Bargaining did not pose any challenge to the achievement of satisfactory effort levels, and managers felt that the elaborate ritual of a joint settlement did much to secure co-operation on the shop floor.

Management also looked upon the union as an effective means of communicating broader messages to workers. For this purpose, the works manager met the shop stewards regularly to present a comparison of their own factory performance against that of others around the company. During one presentation which took place during the course of this study, the works' manager told the shop stewards of the plant's poor performance relative to their counterparts. He produced a large number of statistics to prove it and for the most part the shop stewards listened carefully and sombrely to his message. He left most of them in little doubt about the competitive pressures bearing down upon the organisation and about the way in which the company continuously evaluated their local performance against that achieved by other company plants. The shop stewards left the meeting in the belief that unless there was steady improvement in performance, local jobs would be threatened as the company retained the right to shift production between its various works.

Shop stewards

In such circumstances the shop stewards behaved as a collection of individual delegates rather than a co-ordinated team of representatives with an agreed purpose. Viewing their relations with workers elsewhere as competitive, and with limited scope for developing the extent of bargaining with local management, these were difficult conditions in which to fashion the sorts of 'union principles' (Brown 1973 p.136) which could lead to their working as a team. The convenor (1969–85) provided a vivid account of the stewards' individualist behaviour and more than once alluded to the personal tensions that existed between them:

The Asian stewards only acted on the basis of what their men wanted. Nobody was prepared to stand up and say, 'whether you like it or not, I believe this is the way things should be'. There have been times when I've had to stand and address shop floor meetings when some not-so-friendly shop stewards have spoken against me. It was bloody intimidating. You can't go along with them or you would end up in all sorts of silly situations doing everything that the men want. Eventually what do they want? The moon, the sun, the stars, the whole universe. I had to spell it out to them. Forget it, this is reality! None of them were able to do that. Every time there was trouble ... it was because Asian shop stewards were not strong enough, or they wanted to gain popularity, or they wanted to win re-election. (Convenor 1969–85)

The convenor suppressed the populist stirring of the stewards by calling mass meetings on the shop floor. By all accounts he was a persuasive public speaker and always managed to prevail over his critics, sometimes using his difficult situation to oblige management to grant certain concessions. But his tactics reflected the dilemma in which the local union found itself, trapped within highly centralised control of industrial relations whilst at the same time obliged to give voice to workplace discontent. The curious relationship between the union and the company fostered an atmosphere of mistrust between the convenor and the stewards, and between the stewards themselves. 'Union principles' were stymied by an atmosphere in which suspicions of corruption permeated inter-personal relations:

They [Asian shop stewards] resorted to underhand measures to try to get me out of office, like saying 'the convenor is taking backhanders', which hurt me very much at the time because I was straight, I didn't operate on the principles that they operate ... It is inevitable within the Asian community. As soon as they get any public office they have a tendency to exploit it for their own benefit. Don't ask me why but every

Asian shop steward I came across had a tendency to be like that. If they don't do it on the basis of 'let's have some more overtime', they'll do it on the basis of facilities, having time off or whatever happened to suit them. As soon as it started to happen you could see the rest of the shop stewards watching them and saying, 'well if he can do it, so can I'. It's a bad situation, very unfortunate, but it crept in through the representatives from the Asian community. (Convenor 1969–85)

In more recent times things appeared little changed. The stewards continued to behave in an unco-ordinated and populist fashion, often falling out with each other in pursuit of sectional demands. During this study, several matters arose which took on the character of inter-steward disputes. For example, a dispute arose between two shop stewards about whether some extra overtime should be allocated to either the nightshift or the dayshift workers. Another dispute broke out when one steward claimed that another had informally agreed to reduce the number of staff on a line without consulting him first. And a third, rather more public, dispute took place over changes in staffing levels on a modified production line. In this instance, the plant management was keen to win a special order and adopted a much less lenient attitude towards the number of staff required for the trial period of production. A provisional agreement was duly reached with the dayshift and the eveningshift stewards, but the less accommodating nightshift stewards refused to abide by similar terms. Disagreements and mutual dislike quickly surfaced. The incident could only be settled by the company calling in the union's regional official, who ruled the dispute in favour of the company.

The shop stewards continued to accuse one another privately of accepting bribes from managers. It was commonly alleged that an hour or two of extra overtime pay was regarded as discreet payment for a 'favour'. Junior managers also said that their superiors gave certain stewards favourable treatment in return for co-operation. One of them complained to his boss that the steward working on his line was often absent and rather lazy:

I went to see the personnel manager and asked him if something could be done to discipline the shop steward. He told me not to do anything – because he was useful to us in other ways. (Manager)

It may only have been coincidence that the shop stewards tended to be in the better paid jobs, but some junior managers clearly felt otherwise. They pointed to their superior's decision to employ a shop steward on the most highly automated and best paid line in the factory. Staffed by only a handful of people the company had stipulated that each member of the team must have a well above average attendance record. On this criterion, the shop steward was, by his own admission, not suitable for the job:

I was absolutely amazed when I got this job. To this day I don't know why they chose me! (Shop steward)

But not only did a job on the high technology line give the steward more money, it also intimately associated him with the introduction of a programme of technical change which workers felt to be detrimental to their interests (see below). In these ways the position of the union was compromised, and its capacity to fashion a case against management made all the more limited.

In short, the shop stewards behaved as a fragmented collection of individuals rather than a cohesive body with a common purpose. They viewed each other with a degree of rivalry and mistrust, in part fostered by the highly informal management policy of providing various types of preferential treatment, and in part the consequence of their own cultural and personal differences. Although individual shop stewards sometimes made life difficult for management, the local union was incapable of developing a co-ordinated challenge to management plans.

Workers

Workers watched the gradual process of automation and felt powerless to stop it. For the past twenty years they had offered no resistance to the company in making whatever improvements it felt necessary. Their co-operation had preserved the favoured position of their own plant and their own jobs in the past. But now, the job cuts were of a different magnitude. It was no longer just a matter of losing one or two people off a line but in the most extreme cases the introduction of new equipment meant reducing each line from around twenty people to just three or four. They felt there was little they could do. They had not supported the other factories when they were being closed or rationalised. And one of their own shop stewards, one of three employees on a labour-saving line, had become a symbol of the changes which lay ahead. The workers believed that the company's policy of gradually replacing the existing lines with fully automated ones meant only one thing: that they would lose their jobs.

Nearly two-thirds of the shop floor workforce (63 per cent, $N = 180$) believed that their employment within the next five years was either 'not very secure' or 'not at all secure'. Extensive calculations of the likely savings which the company would make by introducing further automation was a morbid preoccupation on the shop floor. Few workers saw any positive benefit to themselves from the modernisation programme (see table 4.1). Many also felt disappointment at their earnings and long hours of work. Around half (54 per cent) of the full time workers regarded their wages as

Table 4.1 *Which of the following comes closest to your feelings on the new technology being introduced at this factory?*

	% of respondents
Good for the company and the workers	**10**
Good for the company but not the workers	**78**
Not good for the company or the workers	**12**
	$N = 166$

'not too good' or 'very poor'. Even managers admitted that wages were lower than those paid in similar factories in the neighbourhood. Yet what is striking is that these obvious grounds for complaint were never focused into a distinct set of demands, nor did they impair the generally positive and constructive relations which existed between managers and workers.

Despite the degree of close supervision, and squabbles about 'favouritism' on the part of chargehands, managers and workers saw their relations as friendly and co-operative. They incorporated within their relations an expectation that they should behave politely towards each other, avoiding harsh words and direct instructions. Senior management encouraged line managers to avoid tough discipline and confrontation when dealing with individual workers because it felt it could achieve more through a polite approach:

This is an easy factory to manage ... We tend to soft pedal a bit and don't push things through too hard. We don't calculate manning and enforce breaks rigorously because productivity is already fairly high. (Senior manager)

Similarly, workers believed that if managers required them to do some additional tasks, they should ask them for 'a favour' in a polite way. Managers understood this and went about their work in the belief that they should make a conscious effort to get on with their subordinates. Relations between managers and workers were therefore conducted within 'a culture of politeness'. Managers who knew how to operate within the culture believed they could elicit substantial co-operation from workers. Those who could not had a more difficult time. One afternoon, a young manager widely disliked on the shop floor for his 'arrogant attitude' buried his face in his hands and moaned,

I don't know what it is but I just can't get through to these people. (Line manager)

He knew that his failure to manage within 'the culture of politeness' was making him less effective as a manager.

Managers frequently praised workers for their willingness to work flexibly as the need arose:

If we went by the book, this place would never run! (Foreman)

Managers secured individual acts of co-operation with informal payments for 'unofficial' overtime. For example, a machine driver might cover an additional machine in the absence of a colleague and for this he would receive several extra hours of pay at overtime rates. On other occasions management would offer generous amounts of overtime to cover duties to be performed for part of the following shift. Workers' willingness to provide such co-operation, or 'favours' as they were generally known, was of great benefit to management. The alternative was perhaps to leave a particular line idle for a shift and redeploy workers around the rest of the plant at some cost to efficiency. Instead lines often operated with one or two fewer staff than was formally agreed and were rarely halted because of unexpected staff absence. And when dirty, unpleasant, or extra work was required, managers showed their appreciation of workers' co-operation with informal payments.

The practice of 'favours' and 'unofficial overtime' served further to discreetly reinforce workers' commitment to discipline and flexibility. When workers refused to co-operate managers usually responded not by pressing formal discipline upon them, but by offering opportunities for 'favours' to other workers instead. For example, one day the process foreman offered extra overtime to a process worker to cover for shortages elsewhere in the department. He asked him to go and stack cases in the packing hall. It was a hot afternoon and it was a rather arduous task. The worker refused, claiming he had exemption from heavy work. The foreman disputed this, allocated the work to someone else, and the operator went home losing the chance of 4 hours' overtime pay. The foreman's policy was to present the same operator with the same job the next time it arose, until in the end the operator did it because he could no longer afford to sacrifice further overtime earnings. From the foreman's point of view, this ensured that workers were always prepared to be flexible about the 'favours' they provided, doing less pleasant jobs as and when they were required.

The 'culture of politeness' and the associated practice of paying for 'favours' was an informal accommodation which senior managers supported because, on balance, they believed it could secure a high degree of co-operation from workers. Yet although these practices were instigated by management, and although they tended to reinforce management prerogatives, the arrangement worked well precisely because it generated a set of mutual obligations. These obligations served to reconcile managers' and workers' expectations of the employment relation. It was, in certain respects, similar to the 'indulgency pattern' illustrated by Gouldner (1955), in which a network of shared informal understandings between managers and workers provided the basis for harmonious industrial relations. In similar vein, the informal nature of 'unofficial overtime' was seen by workers as recompense for extending individual 'favours' to management beyond normal working practice. They judged the principle of paying for 'favours' as a fair one, and subject to an informally agreed 'going rate' according to the burden of extra duties.

Yet insofar as the system of 'favours' and the 'culture of politeness' were sustained by a belief in certain mutual obligations, they did not offer management straightforward influence on the shop floor. Brown (1973) observed that where workers were offered little opportunity for bargaining, they attempted to develop and extend the customary inducements which management offered in order to gain their co-operation. For similar reasons the 'going rate' for 'favours' had been on an upward trend for some weeks. Workers began to exploit the legitimacy of an existing practice by bidding up the price of their co-operation with management. They took the view that when faced with the relatively low marginal cost of a 'favour' to keep the lines running, management would on any rational basis concede their demand. Things came to a head when one afternoon a line manager asked a process worker to mind an adjacent machine and offered him two hours extra overtime pay. The worker refused and demanded five extra hours to do the job.

When the department manager heard about the incident he quickly realised what was happening. Managers were reporting other problems too. Standards of timekeeping, attendance and job performance were slipping:

At five o'clock, when the evening shift is supposed to start work, I went out onto one of my lines and nobody was there! (Line manager)

The 'culture of politeness' posed a problem. Whilst it could function as an effective means to high levels of productivity, it also tended to constrain management attempts to maintain discipline. Informal arrangements were slowly developing in ways which inhibited management's ability to control the shop floor. Junior managers expressed a degree of frustration about the extent to which politeness sometimes prevented them from tackling problems of poor discipline:

Things aren't as bad as they were five years ago, but if the crunch comes we know senior management won't support us. (Junior manager)

Senior management therefore took a decision to 'tighten-up' in areas where it had previously adopted a lenient attitude, and it forbade 'unofficial overtime' payments.

Managers continued their 'tightening-up' by outlawing the longstanding and widespread practice of 'mutual clocking' by process workers on certain shifts. One evening, without prior discussion, two managers took the dayshift clock cards out of the racks, and handed them to each worker individually at the end of the shift. In a single evening management had taught a lesson to a troublesome shop steward and eliminated the longstanding custom of finishing early. Management 'tightened-up' on the packing lines too. It began a policy of replacing the chargehands with a higher grade of supervisor with greater disciplinary powers. Line managers were also instructed to take a tougher attitude towards absence. It was widely accepted amongst the largely female packers that their domestic responsibilities gave them just reason for not coming to work. The rate of absences fluctuated according to the incidence of school holidays. Although in the past management had not officially accepted domestic responsibilities as a reason for absence, it had avoided questioning workers too closely about their reasons for staying away from work. In future, however, it wanted things to be different. At the start of each shift line managers consulted the new 'absence computer' and began to ask workers returning from a spell of absence about their reasons for staying away from work.

Workers were generally very annoyed by managers' attempts to eliminate traditional working practices. They complained about the 'attitudes' of certain managers, and accused them of showing a 'lack of politeness'. They made defiant statements about how they would make life difficult for 'arrogant' managers:

He won't listen to you, he just orders you about. I told him to stop because if he didn't I'd fuck him up. He said, 'you can't', and I said, 'I can. I can send burnt biscuits down all day if I want to'. (Worker)

Managers quickly became aware that their actions had 'soured attitudes'. The way in which they had outlawed 'mutual clocking' had so offended the process workers that they insisted that the convenor speak directly to the more senior of the two managers who had removed the clock cards from the rack. Soon afterwards, the manager concerned thought it wise to apologise to the process men for his behaviour that evening. Although a number of workers were successfully disciplined for burning biscuits, managers judged that asserting their authority in such an open manner had been to the detriment of workers' morale. Similarly, the introduction of stricter absence records did not help managers to discover why packers chose not to come to work:

If it's personal then I wouldn't tell managers because it gives them a hold over you. (Worker)

Some managers doubted the wisdom of their actions in 'tightening-up' as the feeling grew within the department that production was no longer as successful as it might otherwise have been. Within a few weeks managers started to make unofficial overtime payments once again and tended not to enquire too closely about workers' reasons for being absent.

Yet the 'tightening-up' was also in part successful in communicating a management expectation to workers that more was required of them. Mutual clocking did not regularly take place any more as workers stayed by their machines right until the end of shifts. Whether burnt biscuits were the result of deliberate sabotage or 'spoiling' (Nichols and Beynon 1977), or simply the spread of 'a couldn't care less attitude', management had successfully made clear to workers that their behaviour was not acceptable. Oven operators took greater care over the quality of biscuits. Packers realised that management would no longer be quite so lenient about absence and timekeeping in future. And even although unofficial overtime appeared again, workers were somewhat disabused of the belief that they might bargain with management about the price of 'favours'. Despite the importance of 'polite relations', management had successfully curtailed unhelpful aspects of informality. When a policy of 'leniency' which had previously promoted high productivity started to have the reverse effect, management was able to reassert its authority over workplace behaviour with a fair degree of success.

Management intervention had this effect because workers largely accepted its right to manage (Armstrong et al 1981). A senior manager declared that unofficial overtime payments were,

a discretionary gesture on our part, not a right. (Senior manager)

In his view, exchanges of 'favours' constituted arrangements made between individual workers and managers, even although they were subject to various mutually accepted norms about their circumstances and magnitude. There was little workers could do to challenge this view because it contained aspects of undeniable truth. Their 'favours' in return for 'unofficial overtime' payments were essentially a series of ad hoc individual arrangements made without any formal collective agreement. Since they were exchanged without consultation with shop stewards, there was no union case against their removal. It was not legitimate for the shop stewards to get involved in aspects of management–worker relations which were, quite literally, none of their business.

Workers also accepted management's moral authority to modify other aspects of workplace custom such as slack timekeeping or going home early. They found it difficult to fashion arguments against management even when management's behaviour caused them considerable inconvenience. The significant feature of their complaint against 'tightening-up' was that they protested about management's disregard for politeness rather than disputing management's right to determine their conditions of work. If the development of custom was an expression of a frustrated desire to bargain, its elimination was a significant indication of workers' powerlessness to influence management.

The informal system of 'favours' and the 'culture of politeness' promoted productivity through the creation of a constructive working environment. But as the balance between enhanced co-operation and impaired efficiency was tipped in favour of the latter, management intervened to reassert its right to manage. In the short run 'tightening-up' cut against the grain of 'polite relations' and adversely affected performance. In the longer run, both parties' continued support for the 'culture of politeness' formed the basis of management authority, and furthered efficient production.

The politics of incorporation

The company's clear plan for the management of industrial relations, established twenty years beforehand, had achieved a good deal. It had secured extensive management prerogative and encouraged the development of constructive industrial relations. Looking back, a senior executive closely involved with the development of union recognition expressed his satisfaction thus:

The flexibility we got out of recognition was enormous ... we didn't have a single strike or stoppage and overall it didn't cost us any more than was the going rate for wage increases. But because people felt that they had negotiated these increases themselves, they felt they were worth more than they actually were. (Senior executive)

The idea that management can use or 'sponsor' trades unions so successfully for its own ends has had its critics. Batstone, for example, found the idea rather implausible. He argued that management would only support trades unions where trades unions would otherwise have secured recognition by themselves anyway (1984 p.108). And it is quite true that the biscuit company decided to recognise certain trades unions because it was worried that other more militant trades unions might be able to recruit their employees. But this, however, is perhaps all the more reason for evaluating and explaining the degree to which management policies were successful in containing discontent and promoting effort.

Management's success lay partly in the precise nature of the arrangements made for recognition. The strategic ability of trades unions to disrupt production was minimised and opportunities to develop shop floor bargaining were closely circumscribed. By placing the plants in competition with one another the local union organisation was made aware that resisting change would be more costly than agreeing to accept it. This awareness exercised a profound effect upon the character of local relations between management and the union. Local bargaining served to rationalise and legitimise company initiatives rather than allowing the union to alter company plans in their favour. By predisposing the union to accept management prerogative there was little room for the development of independent 'union principles'. Lack of bargaining opportunities stymied the possibility of stewards making the transition from delegates into leaders, a transition reckoned to be essential for the functioning of effective steward organisation (Batstone 1977). In private, managers judged the stewards, 'a right shower', and joked about the way in which they fell out with each other and undermined each other's efforts. Although managers do not normally have high opinions of shop stewards, at the biscuit works their views had little to do with any personal dislike or prejudice. The stewards' erratic and individual espousal of popular causes made little headway, and sometimes resulted in their becoming isolated and vulnerable to management pressures.

Why did workers continue to support a management and a union that offered them, in their own estimation, relatively little in material terms? They recognised the weak position of the union, and some of them openly alleged that it was 'a company union' which lived 'in the pocket of the management'. But they looked upon the state of competition between plants and the introduction of labour-saving technology as the inevitable product of circumstances beyond their control. On account of this, they saw a distinction between the causes of their general situation and the behaviour of individual persons on the shop floor. Workers pinned their worries on 'the company' rather than on managers, and they blamed 'the union' rather than the shop stewards for not doing anything about them. This suggests that the relationship between workers and their representatives can be more complex than critics of sponsorship have been willing to acknowledge. For example, Harris (1987) suggested that shop stewards who are obliged to serve management interests cannot simultaneously act as spokespersons for their constituents. This point is, however, too simple to capture understanding of the situation as a whole. It is not entirely wrong, for on one occasion in the past a hard line caucus was nearly successful in gaining enough shop floor support to depose the convenor on account of his support for company policy. In practice, however, the tensions present in relations between the company, the union and its members were surmountable. Management, in this instance as in others, successfully 'managed the contradictions' (Nichols and Beynon 1977 p.130). By agreeing to a prudent wage–concession the company was able to considerably restore the fortunes of the embattled convenor (1969–85) who subsequently became universally remembered as 'the super-hero that got us the paid dinner break'. Managers knew the value of making situations look as if the stewards were trying hard, and on occasions getting somewhere. The willingness of the shop stewards to espouse popular causes, and their visible success in achieving minor (though in reality often artificial) victories over management on matters of staffing and discipline, led around three fifths (62 per cent, $N = 161$) of the shop floor to believe they were doing a reasonably good job of representing their interests. Management was able to influence the judgements which workers made about their representatives through the deliberate manipulation of collective bargaining on the shop floor. Sporadic outbursts of populism were simultaneously both signs of the stewards' weakness and the reason for their enjoying continued shop floor support.

Workers were committed to the culture at the biscuit works because in many ways it met their expectations of work. They valued the 'culture of politeness' in itself, perhaps in part because it provided confirmation that their work was valuable to management. Moreover, although their activities tended to be closely supervised, the continuous business of interpreting workplace rules brought workers into close relationships with managers. The business of modifying rules led to a climate of management by agreement and ensured consistency and fairness in the organisation of work. Bargaining over the price of favours successfully integrated managers' and workers' expectations about the allocation of rewards, establishing a series of moral obligations or contracts between them.

Conclusions

Amidst growing commercial pressures the biscuit company pursued a policy of rationalisation and progressive modernisation of its plants. The introduction of change was managed in a way which elicited high levels of productivity and sustained co-operation from shop floor workers. Rather than attempt either to assert its prerogative or to transform the shop floor with a radical new vision of industrial relations, it relied upon an approach to industrial relations that had been set out some twenty years beforehand when trades unions had first been recognised by the company. A thoughtful embrace of trades unions had proved effective in building a mechanism for channelling grievances away from the shop floor, where their expression might otherwise have restricted production and amicable relations. At the same time, management provided positive assistance in persuading workers that shop stewards shared a degree of its responsibility for making decisions. This involved skilful presentation of the company's interests and clever manipulation of the local union. Of equal importance was the attention which management paid to preserving traditional features of relationships between workers and managers. The 'culture of politeness' which suffused shop floor relations generally served to reinforce management prerogative. On account of the rituals of performing 'favours' and receiving 'unofficial overtime' there was founded an extensive pattern of voluntary and mutual obligations which supported flexible and efficient working practices.

The biscuit works provides managers in industry with a tantalising glimpse of the prospect that there may be more than one model for a 'new industrial relations'. In many respects, the company's approach appeared old-fashioned. The complex hierarchy of managers and supervisors reflected the company's adherence to the principles of scientific management rather than modern prescriptions for autonomous team working. The myriad of status differences which persisted on the shop floor cut against the egalitarian ideals which modernists believe to be important in fashioning common commitment within an organisation. Elaborate procedures for representing workers by means of multiple trades unions, complemented by longstanding informal shop floor practices, continued to form an integral part of the management process, where elsewhere such approaches have been judged an important cause of industrial relations breakdown. This success was due in no small part to the sophistication with which traditional measures were managed. The company carefully avoided crude displays of management power and instead skilful management of relations with trades unions incorporated them within a programme of change. Its preference for 'politeness' gave workers a dignity and purpose in their work. Its support for the system of 'favours' recognised differences of interest between workers and managers and found a means to resolve them to a sufficient degree which both parties found satisfactory. As a consequence, these old-fashioned aspects of industrial relations enjoyed a good measure of success in delivering the goals of the 'new industrial relations'. Collective bargaining both diffused dissent and created a climate in which co-operation could develop. Informal arrangements complemented formal collective bargaining as the wage–effort bargain served to foster rather than frustrate a climate of moral involvement in work.

Yet important as these achievements were at the biscuit works, it is also necessary to keep them in perspective. The system of work organisation required continuous and detailed supervision, and although workers co-operated genuinely and extensively with management, their commitment was essentially limited to an exchange of additional effort or flexibility in return for additional pay. Nor was the system entirely stable, as disagreements between the shop stewards sometimes flared up into time consuming problems for management. In these respects management's achievement, whilst more than sufficient for orderly and efficient production, fell short of the standard of worker commitment sought by some enthusiasts of the 'new industrial relations'. In these rather more demanding terms, therefore, the biscuit works might be judged only a qualified success. Some seasoned experts might judge that to ask for more with respect to manual jobs is optimistic, and perhaps even naive. But it may also be the case that where management has considerable freedom to fashion labour relations without the constraint of organised labour, extensive co-operation can engender a deep-seated sense of worker commitment.

Chapter 5 therefore turns attention from union workplaces to non-union workplaces and their attempts to create a sense of moral involvement in work without collective bargaining. It examines life on the shop floor of large non-union works and explores whether, in the absence of unions, management can cultivate a more genuine and open relationship with workers. Is it possible in such an environment to generate a higher degree of common commitment to a common purpose? Have the achievements of sophisticated non-union employers provided a model for the future of industrial relations?

5   The chocolate works

Introduction

The employment policies of prominent non-union companies continue to arouse keen interest. Widely regarded as highly sophisticated, they are often seen as leading the way towards a new style of co-operative industrial relations. The practical appeal of these policies stems from a belief in their potential to resolve differences of interest between management and employees. The innovations made by such companies may have provided the blueprint for the practical development of 'human resource management' in a growing number of businesses.

Several distinctive features of management policy have emerged from the existing accounts of these 'model' organisations. Independent commentators have often identified a 'company philosophy' extolling values which bind members of the organisation together in a common culture (see, for example, Cressey *et al.* 1985). From the point of view of management, Peach (1983) has emphasised the importance of eliminating collective grievances over wages and job security through the provision of excellent salaries and employment prospects, and coping effectively with individual complaints through extensive procedures. Such an approach comprises a series of measures, the combined purpose of which is the creation of a high degree of commitment on the part of workers to the goals of their employer.

Since current thinking in industrial relations may owe an increasing debt to organisations which have pioneered such approaches to their employees, it has become correspondingly more important to cast an enquiring eye over their achievements. The chocolate works which is the subject of this chapter is typical of many large and successful non-union workplaces in Britain and the USA. For several years it has witnessed a determined move away from a style of management typical of many non-union employers in the past, which rested quite explicitly upon an exchange of very high wages in return for high standards of obedience, towards a 'culture of commitment'. The chocolate company developed its own 'company philosop' committed itself to a policy of common status for all employees, repl·

direct supervision with a system of team working, and encouraged the personal development of employees through systems of individual appraisal and company training programmes. All in all, the implementation of these measures constituted an extensive programme of change.

The developments at the chocolate works provide an opportunity to contemplate to what extent, and in what ways, these new initiatives can succeed in modifying employees' attitudes. In particular, this chapter explores workers' views about their own interests in relation to those of the company, and examines the extent to which they were able to express differences of view in the absence of independent representation or spokespersons. There is a particular need for more evidence in this area because what little has been discovered so far has presented an ambiguous picture. For example, Cressey et al. (1985), in a study of an apparently sophisticated non-union factory, suggested that most employees were well disposed towards the organisation and that they endorsed the 'company philosophy' which supported constructive and co-operative working relationships. But equally, the authors believed that the emphasis which management placed upon company values created powerful pressures for conformity, limiting opportunities for employees to express their own views. This idea has been reinforced by evidence from a small survey of workers employed in a similar organisation by Dickson et al. (1988). Here, too, individuals felt discouraged from disagreeing with managers because of the risks attendant upon being labelled a 'troublemaker'. In these circumstances, the possibility that sophisticated new labour relations policies can generate genuine shop floor co-operation must be explored alongside the prospect that such policies exert powerful pressures upon employees, narrowing opportunities for expressing dissent. Following inevitably from such considerations is the issue of whether this brand of industrial relations can bring stability to working relationships, and whether these policies might be replicated elsewhere with success. Can this approach to employee relations constitute the basis of a new and productive model for other workplaces?

A new style of management

The chocolate works was one of several owned by a successful multinational company. In comparison with its competitors, it produced a fairly restricted number of products, generally of simple construction, which were aggressively priced. With very low profit margins per unit of output, the firm's success was accounted for by achieving very high production volumes, a 'Fordist' approach to the production of confectionery. The works had been established during the 1930s and employment reached a peak during the 1970s when it provided jobs for more than 1,500 people. Thereafter, as greater automation was introduced into the plant, the numbers employed fell through natural wastage and early retirement to around 1,000 people at the time this study was made.

As far as it is possible to tell, for many years the management approach to industrial relations at the chocolate works had fostered the idea of the employment relation as a wage–effort bargain. The company made a clear commitment to pay rates at least 10 percent higher than those available at other local workplaces and in return it required workers to maintain high standards of timekeeping, attendance and flexibility. For example, all employees were required to clock-in at the beginning of each shift, and 10 percent of an employee's pay, that is an amount approximating to the premium on other local rates, was dependent upon achieving a 'good timekeeping bonus'. The shop floor was closely supervised by managers, chargehands and 'leading hands'. The premium which raised wages above those prevailing in local union plants enabled the company to insist that workers perform tasks according to production needs, and provided a firm rebuttal in situations where individuals felt disposed to argue about 'job rights'.

Despite premium wages, many workers didn't stay long. An investigation by a team of external consultants, hired during the mid-1950s to investigate the high levels of labour turnover, interviewed 300 production workers and illustrated that managers and supervisors tended towards an autocratic style. Whilst many workers were very satisfied with their wages, and some spoke highly of their managers, others complained of being pushed around by chargehands and of the amount of work that was required. These views, and the similar views of other long-serving managers and workers, conjured up a picture of a management style based upon unilateral application of high standards of effort and discipline in return for high wages. Managers joked about how employees were traditionally required to be no more than 'warm and vertical'. One worker, reflecting upon his early experiences, recollected that 'being in here was like being in the army'. In short, the company's approach to labour relations was typical perhaps of many large non-union employers at the time. It shaped an explicit kind of wage–effort bargain, buying strict obedience to certain rules and high standards of effort with a commitment to maintain premium wages. Workers who didn't like the bargain on offer were given little opportunity to alter its terms, and generally left to seek work elsewhere.

For many years this approach worked reasonably well from the company's point of view. It reflected management's view of shop floor workers as 'hands', capable of acquiring the limited skills necessary for production quite quickly, generally without need for expensive training.

Management enjoyed considerable freedom to manage production with a minimum of employee participation. The number of quits did remain a persistent problem, and sometimes even resulted in labour shortages which restricted production. But on the whole this approach to labour relations was judged well suited to the type of work the company offered, and to the conditions prevailing in the local labour market. A long-serving manager held the view that high levels of labour turnover imposed minimal cost, and within the buoyant local labour market also provided considerable support for management. Since plenty of alternative jobs were available, disaffected workers were inclined to seek employment elsewhere rather than press their grievances within the works.

During the late 1970s, however, the company began to have further thoughts about its traditional approach to labour relations. Its view of employees as 'hands' began to change and it decided that a new and more sophisticated approach to motivating staff was required. A number of factors combined prompted senior management to think about industrial relations in the longer term. The expansion of the company's overseas plants was exerting pressure upon domestic costs. Sophisticated new machinery was gradually being introduced on the production lines which, in order to function successfully, required the attention of workers with more skills and training than in the past. Furthermore the company could no longer confidently rely upon disaffected workers to quit in favour of work elsewhere. Trades unions made several attempts to recruit workers and gain recognition from management. Allegations (unproven) appeared in the local press that the company had sacked union activists and there were unpleasant scenes outside the works which caused some adverse publicity:

At the present time there is no great demand for further involvement [in decision-making] ... but the publicity given to topics such as participation and involvement may well produce an expectancy in our workforce, which if not met, could result in their resorting to a third party. (Internal management discussion paper, c. 1977)

For a time, senior management contemplated the advantages and disadvantages of recognising a union. But it decided, like many other long-established non-union employers, that such a course of action would be too much at odds with the existing culture of the organisation:

Whilst we are in favour of progressing to a more participative style, we do not believe that this is best achieved through the agency of a third party.

Managers looked abroad for new ideas, and in particular to the USA where they visited several large non-union workplaces. Their views, on their return, had clearly been influenced by emerging human resource management techniques. They suggested that the new approach to employee relations should go far beyond management policies of the past. Workers' simple obedience was no longer adequate to ensure the achievement of the highest possible standards of quality and efficiency. Management should devote substantial energies to encouraging a culture of participation through,

involving people in their jobs so that they can improve their contribution, gain job satisfaction and thereby increase the efficiency of the business.

The inclination to adopt ideas and practices from the USA prevailed over those from Europe when management clearly rejected representative forms of participation such as Works Councils. Management believed that elected workplace representatives could,

reduce and in some cases replace the role of the line manager as a communicator and representative of his people.

Furthermore they felt that a workers' representative body might,

reduce the degree of organisational flexibility [and] . . . readily become a negotiating body which could, in the course of a dispute, have recourse to a third party.

To avoid such difficulties, the company decided that the purpose of a new management style should be to develop an environment in which workers identified more directly with the aims of the business rather than to develop representative institutions which might declare their independence from management.

During the early 1980s management began to build the new culture by taking initiatives in three areas. First, it developed a formal 'company philosophy'; second, it established new methods of working with a view to encouraging workers to accept greater responsibility for production; and third, it developed an elaborate new system of remuneration intended to reward commitment and flexibility. The new approaches to working methods and rewards were embodied in aspects of the 'Company Principles', which are described below.

New values

Senior management believed that the new approach to employee relations should be founded upon an explicit set of moral values whose purpose was to bind the organisation together in a clear set of shared beliefs. 'The Principles' opened with statements about the importance of satisfying the demands of the consumer by producing products of the highest possible quality:

Each individual sale must be regarded as our most important sale . . . we must regard the consumer as our boss; the consumers' needs and desires are the reasons why our product is chosen or rejected. By every means available we must seek to discover what these needs are, so that we can shape our products to satisfy them ... Quality products, perceived as having fine ingredients and consistently meeting standards of excellence, will attract consumers, confirm their right decision and attract them again. (Extract from the company principle of Quality)

They explained the importance of both accepting and sharing a broader range of responsibilities within the organisation:

We choose to be different from those corporations where many layers of management dilute the sense of responsibility. Our employees are asked to take on direct and total responsibility for results, exercising initiative and making decisions as their tasks require ... Every employee has an important contribution to make toward our success ... In recognition of our mutual contributions, we regard all employees in an equal light and avoid divisive privileges. In return for accepting responsibility, employees are rewarded in salaries and benefits that are above average. (Statement of the company principle of Responsibility)

They continued by drawing attention to the importance of efficiency:

Sometimes, our beliefs invite disbelief. How is it possible to pay above-average wages, maintain superior value for money and freely share our success? Our strength lies in our efficiency – the ability to organise all our assets for maximum productivity and minimum waste, so that our products are produced at the lowest possible cost .... efficiency makes all other things possible. (Statement of the company principle of Efficiency)

The essential message contained within the 'Company Principles' was that members of the organisation should always strive to produce products of high quality by the most efficient means, and that they should be allowed to exercise appropriate degrees of responsibility in order to make this possible. With each individual committed to the Principles, with each member of the organisation making a contribution to the well-being of others, each should be accorded equal dignity by means of similar status.

A common approach to rewards

According to the company, the mutual dividend for adherence to 'the Principles' was the continued success of the company and maintenance of above-average pay. It believed that the Principles should inform the basis of everyday thinking and decision-making within the organisation. To this end, senior management expressed commitment to the attainment of an 'egalitarian culture', embodied in the principle of 'Responsibility', by means of a variety of symbolic measures. For example, managers continued to clock-in and receive their wages on a weekly basis just like production workers. They also worked in open-plan offices and all employees shared common canteen facilities. The senior management valued these rather idiosyncratic policies because they felt that they symbolised to all members of the organisation that 'the contribution' of each individual to the functioning of the organisation was of equal importance. The only difference that existed between them was their rate of pay, and in terms of the thinking behind the Principles, this was a reflection of the different levels of responsibility which individuals were obliged to bear.

Senior management gave further practical expression to this idea by devising a uniform approach to motivation which incorporated every member of the organisation. The separate job grading systems for blue collar workers, white collar workers, and management were combined into a single extended hierarchical scale upon which individual jobs were measured according to common principles. Incentive schemes which previously had been applicable only to management were extended to include shop floor workers. For example, a pay bonus scheme which reflected the company's 'return on total assets', previously paid only to managers, was henceforth included in shop floor pay packets. By introducing an element of profit-related pay into the wages of every worker, the company emphasised to employees their personal responsibility for company performance. It wanted to make shop floor workers think about how their behaviour on the shop floor affected the performance of the company *vis-à-vis* its competitors. At the same time, and for good measure, senior management announced that there would be no further cost-of-living pay increases. From henceforth pay increases for every employee would depend upon the performance of the organisation.

In truth, the principles by which management pay was determined were not quite identical to the means by which pay was settled for other employees. For example, the 'return on total assets' bonus continued to comprise a larger proportion of management than of shop floor pay. Nor were merit pay awards extended to shop floor workers (because line managers felt that it would be difficult to justify such payments to the majority of workers not favoured to receive them). Nevertheless, these minor differences apart, the company developed a common approach to rewards in the belief that it would both foster awareness of the competitive position of the business and bind individuals together in the common pursuit of higher standards.

A new approach to flexibility

New management beliefs about the ways in which workers could be motivated more effectively were also reflected in new approaches to organising work. The company was committed to improving productivity and participation, not simply by introducing incentive schemes but also by requiring individuals to take greater responsibility for improving their own results. The traditional approach to labour relations, which required that workers obediently accept the minute direction of chargehands, gave way to a situation in which direct supervision was eliminated. Workers were expected to organise their own activities over an increasingly wide range of tasks. Management believed that efficiency could be continuously improved by focusing the energies and imagination of shop floor workers upon the primary purpose of the organisation as contained in 'the Principles': production at the highest possible quality by the most cost-effective means.

Management expressed this message by altering the division of labour on the shop floor in other ways. It wanted to supplant the idea that workers' obligations lay within performing a narrow function, or practising a particular skill, and promote the idea that workers should use all their available talents to advance production. To this end, the specialist maintenance department, once home to an elite group of skilled workers, was disbanded and the fitters were sent to production lines where they were no longer engaged solely in repairing machines but also in various production tasks. Production workers were, by the same token, encouraged (after appropriate training) to perform minor maintenance for themselves with a view to encouraging them to keep their machines continuously at the peak of efficiency. The quality assurance department experienced a similar fate and its duties were also transferred to workers on the production line. Management believed that by reorganising activities in these ways the attitudes and behaviour of employees would enable continuous improvements in the quality and efficiency of production.

Changes in the division of labour and in the rewards system gave rise to a distinctive approach to grading and promotion which extended from the most junior to the most senior members of the organisation. Shop floor manual workers (who would be regarded in rather old-fashioned terms as unskilled, semi-skilled and skilled employees), occupied the lowest four grades in the reward structure. Their grades were further divided into five sub-divisions, making a total of around 20 effective levels of manual employee. Under the new 'pay-for-knowledge' arrangements individuals who improved their flexibility and effectiveness by successfully completing company training courses moved upwards through the grading structure. Progression through each sub-division of each grade entitled an individual to an increase in pay.

The character of management initiatives
The new management style reflected senior management's changing beliefs about the relationship between industrial relations and competitive

performance. The traditional style of management autocracy in return for premium wages gave way to a more sophisticated approach. Management integrated explicit philosophical principles with new motivation techniques and practical developments in work organisation. The purpose of the changes was to create an environment in which individuals could feel that their own efforts were contributing both to their own success and to the success of the wider organisation.

The new approach sought to promote co-operation by removing from the shop floor every suggestion of a division of interests between shop floor workers and the company. Management's aim was no longer to subordinate workers by means of premium wages, but to create the basis for management by agreement founded upon a set of mutual beliefs about the way in which the organisation should function. In place of a firm distinction between the company, as represented by management, and the shop floor, the purpose of the Company Principles was to engender the perception that seniority was allocated on the basis of wider responsibilities. In turn, these reflected broader competencies and expertise, channelled in the pursuit of common goals.

Yet despite its apparent sophistication, the new approach carefully preserved traditional management values and freedoms. The principles of 'Efficiency' and 'Quality' supported customary management goals, whilst 'Responsibility' incorporated decision-making within a hierarchy controlled by management. It was to be extended to workers only in ways which did not weaken the right of seniors to manage subordinates in the pursuit of whatever business goals were necessary to secure 'Quality' and 'Efficiency'. For example, the company's determination to secure high standards of job performance was reflected in management's control over the 'pay-for-knowledge' system. Access to training was at the discretion of line managers who selected employees on the basis of their displaying positive attitudes. And the company's traditional insistence upon high standards of timekeeping and attendance was carried over to the 'pay-for-knowledge' system. Even when an individual passed a training course, confirmation of a subsequent grade increase was dependent upon that individual meeting the company standard, which was decided by management alone. Furthermore, representative structures of employee participation were eschewed because they threatened a divisive break within the hierarchy of responsibilities. Instead, the well-being of individual workers was the responsibility of line managers whose duty was,

to represent the company to the people and his [the manager's] people's views to the company. As the leader of a work group, he is the person with whom any employee can most easily identify. This is encouraged by his accessibility . . . and the small size of the work group which averages about 20 to 30 people . . . the free exchange of views is encouraged by the absence of physical or status barriers. (Evidence submitted by the firm to the Royal Committee of Inquiry on Industrial Democracy, 1977)

The new management style therefore remained essentially unitarist although the symbolism with which it was endowed, and the techniques with which it was enacted, were more sophisticated than in the past. Whilst its aim was to bind workers and managers together by emphasising their common interest in securing certain goals, control over broad aspects of decision-making remained a management prerogative. Other than face to face briefing sessions called by managers, workers were not granted an independent method of agreeing or challenging management decisions.

Given management's unitarist premise, the interesting question is the extent to which this new management style succeeded in encouraging workers' initiative. From the point of view of workers, did the new industrial relations policies promote an altogether different view of the employment relation, or did they simply increase the pressures placed upon them to conform to the company's expectations of high performance? In what ways, and to what extent, did the new initiatives in practice create an agreed basis for management?

On the shop floor

Most of the study period at the chocolate works was spent observing two adjacent production lines which produced several million bars of chocolate covered toffee every week. The production process on each line was divided into three stages. First, large quantities of toffee were produced by four men in charge of a large continuous process. They periodically made fine judgements about the varying mix of temperatures and pressures necessary to maintain the toffee at an appropriate consistency. Second, in the middle of the production line, the toffee was continuously cut into pieces which formed bar centres which were then enrobed with chocolate. Generally there were three workers on each of the two mid-line stations, making a total of six. Finally, in the wrapping room, the finished bars were wrapped and packed into boxes. In the wrapping room there were three different kinds of job. Machine operators controlled the fully automated wrapping machines on one line. These machines both wrapped sweets and packed them into boxes. The operators' main duties were to clear and re-start the machines when sweets got jammed inside their mechanisms. On the other line, a team of three packers worked on each semi-automated machine, two packing whilst the other relieved and cleaned. A number of machine engineers, some of whom were former maintenance fitters, were not attached to any one particular machine and were charged with the general

Table 5.1 *Under the new 'pay-for-knowledge' system, there no longer existed 'a rate for the job' but workers in each area tended to occupy the following grades:*

Process	
Process operators	grade 2 or 3
Mid-line	
Guillotine and enrober operators	grade 2 or 3
Wrapping room	
Packers and machine operators	grade 1
Quality checkers	grade 2
Machine engineers	grade 2, 3, 4

duty of making sure that all the wrapping machines operated efficiently, repairing them when they broke down. Two other employees were employed on each shift to perform continuous quality checks on the finished products. Their work involved the constant repetition of simple and routine tests upon the size and weight of finished bars. Approximately 70 workers were employed on each of the three daily shifts. Two line managers on each shift were responsible for the production lines (see table 5.1).

New values in production

It soon became evident that management put the new company philosophy into practice with the intention of encouraging workers to adopt the values of 'Responsibility', 'Quality', and 'Efficiency' in all that they did.

To awaken workers to the belief that they themselves were responsible for improving performance, management refrained from direct supervision of work. Managers generally accorded workers considerable autonomy and work routines were often organised on the basis of customs devised amongst workers themselves. For example, in the process and mid-line, managers believed that operators should run the plant on the basis of their own experience. Sometimes several shifts would pass without a visit from the manager. Left to their own devices, the process operators worked out their own pattern of working and determined their own breaks. When things were running smoothly only one or two remained in the control room whilst the others would spend their time in the canteen. When things were going badly they would work through their breaks to sort out problems. A similar situation existed in the wrapping room where groups of packers rotated around the semi-automated wrapping machines, spending three days on each. This practice equalised their expenditure of effort, as machines towards the end of the line took less sweets. Management preferred to instil motivation by indirect means, for example, in the regular 'housekeeping audits'. Each week an 'independent' manager from elsewhere in the works was asked to review the cleanliness and the tidiness of the production floor. His report was pinned to the notice board, with marks out of ten and detailed comments, providing both praise and criticism. Management believed that doing things in this way allowed workers to take responsibility upon themselves for achieving high standards.

On occasions when things did go wrong managers generally adopted a positive approach. For example, mid-line operators were being assisted by a worker sent from the wrapping room by the manager. This worker was cleaning one of the toffee guillotines with a steam hose when the hose got caught up in the guillotine damaging both the blade and the steam hose irreparably. The line stopped and the mid-line crew were summoned to the manager's office. The manager explained,

They [the mid-line crew] hadn't explained the job properly to him. The way we solved this was to get the four guys into the office, not the guy who made the mistake. They were worried about what was going to happen to them, but instead I said that we should make sure this never happens again. So they agreed in future that they would explain the job better. (Line manager)

The manager adopted a corrective rather than a punitive approach to discipline: his actions were deliberately intended to encourage workers to do better in the future, rather than punish them for what they had done wrong in the past. In this way line managers preferred to 'develop the potential' of their workers to take responsibility and manage problems for themselves. They would devise projects for workers to undertake, generally to do with improving efficiency, or they would encourage them to go on training courses to improve their skills and flexibility.

From the company's point of view, this new thinking went hand in glove with new emphasis on 'Quality'. The quality checkers on each shift were given powers to stop particular machines, or even the entire production line, if they encountered production that repeatedly deviated from specification. On a small number of occasions, quality checkers had taken such measures even though line managers openly disagreed with their decision. In each of these instances, senior management supported the quality checkers' actions and informally reprimanded line managers for disputing their judgement. Senior management believed that their behaviour had demonstrated the belief that blind obedience to management was secondary to encouraging workers' intrinsic commitment to secure high standards.

Things looked rather different from the workers' point of view. Management's approach, however indirect, exerted continuous pressure. Workers knew that the housekeeping audit brought poor areas to the attention of their manager. Similarly although the process men said that their manager rarely paid them much attention, equally they never knew when he might turn up, just to see how things were going:

The manager came back to-day (after a few days off) and he came up to see us, looking round everywhere, checking that everything was alright. (Worker)

Although these encounters were generally relaxed affairs, beneath their appearance of informality most workers understood the importance of showing a 'good attitude'. Not only could managers ask an individual to help out anywhere else on the line, they could move a person from one job to another (broadly within the same grade) permanently. It was common knowledge that workers who had displayed 'negative attitudes' in the past had sometimes been shifted to less pleasant jobs, where they were less able to spread their opinions to other workers. The process crew grumbled about the new quality control procedures which, from their point of view, meant more work and more responsibility:

All the time, they're trying to cut us down up here. It's their decision. I will do what I can do. But that over there [pointing to the new machinery for testing product moisture content] is just the start of it. All the time extra work and no extra money. (Worker)

Similarly, the incident on the mid-line station in which the steam hose was damaged was viewed less positively by workers than by managers. It impressed upon workers the idea that even though damage to the plant was a consequence of the company's unwillingness to provide trained cover, they were nonetheless expected to assume additional responsibility for an untrained employee and the performance of the line, regardless of their being shorthanded.

Pressures to improve flexibility and efficiency often manifested themselves in more obvious ways. Management reserved the right to alter customary ways of working whenever necessary. Concessions once granted by management to ease work pressures were sometimes eliminated in a drive to cut costs. For example, when a longstanding arrangement to provide additional overtime cover on a small chocolate line was rescinded, the workload of the remaining operators was increased. Managers also redeployed labour as they felt necessary at the beginning of each shift and workers often did not perform tasks normally associated with their particular grade. On some shifts, packers were sometimes sent to watch the toffee guillotines on the mid-line if one of the crews happened to be shorthanded. Machine engineers sometimes found themselves performing the role of machine operators or packing sweets. It was therefore commonplace for workers' customary ways of working to be altered in an instant by an instruction from management. And although workers were often not happy about changing jobs, they generally accepted that they had little choice but to obey the manager.

Managers took the view that effort standards were at their discretion. They said that formal staffing standards resulted in a lack of flexibility and created a barrier to improvement. Instead, managers individually determined the organisation of their shift and some adopted the practice of running their shifts with fewer people. As a rule, managers did not cover for inevitable sickness, holidays, and absence with proportionate amounts of overtime. For example, when a line manager allocated one of his process crew to a project on waste reduction, his colleagues were obliged to cover for the absence. The remaining operators were not consulted prior to the change and they did not know whether this amounted to a permanent reduction in their numbers. Similarly, line speeds were varied by managers in accordance with the demand for sweets, with a view to minimising the holding of stock. Increasing the speed of the line had direct effects in the wrapping room. One day, after receipt of a big order, a shift manager revealed,

The line is running faster today than it has ever run before and we've got two wrapping machines out! (Line manager)

Two wrapping machines were out of operation because there were insufficient numbers of people on the shift to crew them. As more sweets were wrapped on fewer machines, the speed of each wrapping machine was increased and packers had to work more quickly to keep up.

In making the decision to run with fewer staff, some managers implicitly adopted a tougher approach to labour relations:

There are arguments between packers and machine engineers to do with the fact that the previous shift pack slower ... so the packers argue, why should we have to work more quickly. (Line manager)

One of the managers was of the view that conflict was the result of machine engineers being 'weak' and intimidated by packers. He said that 'strong' machine engineers encountered few problems, because they could 'command respect'. Personality clashes apart, however, it was the case that relations between packers and the machine engineers became strained when managers were trying to push packing speeds to the limit. Packers were not always willing to work harder in order to meet orders, and argued with the machine engineers:

We used to have one chargehand but now we have six. The machine engineers are trying to take charge. They tell you to work on another machine, or to go and relieve somebody. If they tell you to do something you can't say no because they'll go and see the manager. He will always back them up. (Worker)

Arguments usually stopped short of the manager's office. When a manager did become involved, however, he intervened decisively as packers had suggested on behalf of the machine engineers. A line manager explained his usual approach as follows:

I start by asking them [the packers] if they think the machine engineer's request is reasonable, then I get into the contractual bit [about obeying all reasonable instructions]. (Line manager)

More often arguments rumbled on beneath the surface. The packers saw little purpose in persisting with their complaints and machine engineers did not like to exhibit weakness to their manager. Sometimes these disputes involved minor but persistent effort restriction by packers. For example, the amount of time it took packers to change rolls of wrapping paper or clear jammed sweets, during which time their machine was stopped, depended greatly upon their enthusiasm. When relations with the machine engineers were poor, packers took longer about these things and the inevitable consequence was a marginal reduction in efficiency. On one shift some of the packers escalated their action and turned down the speeds of their wrapping machines. Once again, when news of this behaviour reached the manager he responded decisively by instructing the machine engineers to check the speeds of each wrapping machine once an hour. But although some of the machine engineers did as their manager asked, others were reticent about doing so. Obeying the management's instruction made their relations with the packers all the more difficult. And within a culture in which all individuals were supposed to accept responsibility for their own efforts, and be directly accountable to their line manager, the basis of their authority was often disputed by the packers:

Some of the machine engineers try it on but we just tell them where to go. (Worker)

As things turned out, the course of action recommended by the manager was ineffective. Machine engineers were often busy and it was hard to catch recalcitrant packers in the act of interfering with machines:

Machine engineers handled the situation at the start of the shift, but if machines were turned down during the shift then I moved in and made things very clear. Real head to head stuff, telling them that it wasn't on, what the production standards were, and why they were important. (Line manager)

Soon afterwards a more direct solution to the problem emerged. The dials indicating the number of sweets wrapped per minute were removed from machines, and the speed controls were locked with keys held only by the machine engineers.

These events illustrate the tensions that arose on the shop floor over appropriate standards of effort, both in times of heavy demand and as a consequence of management's relentless drive to improve efficiency. They also reveal how managers had the power to raise effort levels even where workers were not similarly committed to doing so. Some managers made use of this power more than others through a deliberate decision to run their lines with as few staff as possible. They relied upon their authority to overcome arguments as they arose. Such differences of view amongst managers coincided with other differences in their practical interpretation of the 'Company Principles'.

Whilst it was generally the case that managers dealt positively with workers who they felt had made genuine mistakes, and took tougher action against workers who tried to restrict their effort, managers tended to interpret situations differently. Some clearly believed that there was greater merit in a punitive approach to discipline. For example, when towards the end of a shift the process operators failed to close a valve, the wrong recipe was dispensed. The problem continued to be undetected by the incoming shift for an hour and a half despite the process crew's awareness of quality problems further up the line. The managers on both shifts agreed to discipline their process crews for poor job performance, with the incoming crew receiving a reprimand one procedural degree less severe than the outgoing crew. But when the manager of the outgoing shift imposed only a relatively minor sanction upon his workers, the managers of the incoming shift were surprised and dismayed. They tried to persuade him to increase the severity of the penalty but he declined, and later he tried to justify his position by explaining as follows:

Part of the culture round here is to slap on a warning as soon as someone steps out of line. But I don't believe in retribution. It's at odds with encouraging people to take responsibility. (Line manager)

This 'part of the culture' had its roots in the traditional approach to industrial relations which pre-dated the new initiatives.

Traditional discipline manifested itself in other ways too, through 'decrees from on high' which were sometimes issued in order to put an immediate stop to disorderly situations. For example, the works manager arrived on the morning of a visit from the company's most senior management to discover that some nightshift workers had gone home early. The shift change had been poor and in the changing rooms dirty overalls were strewn across the floor. He immediately issued an instruction: anybody found anywhere other than on their line during the first and last hour of a shift would be punished with a written warning, unless they had received express permission from their line manager. Throughout the duration of a warning, workers lost their entitlement to company performance bonuses or pay increases on promotion. In a profitable year their expected pay might be reduced by anything between £200 and £1,000. Senior management intended to impose stiff punishments on offenders.

Some managers expressed semi-private disagreement with this punishment-centred approach to rule-making. Others defended the works manager's decision. They accused offenders of 'basically saying to their managers that they don't have enough authority to keep them on the line' and by leaving dirty overalls lying around, of 'showing insufficient respect for the company'. Whatever their personal views, managers issued a spate of warnings within the first few weeks of the new 'first and last hour' rule being in force. Some admitted that they had punished good workers with quite reasonable excuses who had simply forgotten to gain permission in advance. This was an indiscriminate rule, introduced without consultation, and it served as a clear message to the shop floor that the wishes of management ought to be respected on pain of summary discipline.

Most workers thought that the 'first and last hour' rule was 'silly' and 'unfair'. Some of them believed that having to ask the manager's permission to go to the toilet was demeaning and incompatible with the responsibilities that they were encouraged to exercise in their work. After a decent interval, some managers let it become known that they too disliked the rule. They found it inconvenient and tiresome to spend two hours of each day making sure their staff did not slip away without permission and, moreover, they sensed that shop floor relations were not as friendly as they had been before the rule was introduced. These more progressive managers believed that it had brought little useful benefit and within a relatively short time the 'first and last hour' rule became practically redundant. Workers spoke favourably of managers that didn't enforce the rule. Yet workers also knew that the rule remained available for use at some point in the future at the discretion of individual managers. The 'decree' was a symbol of management authority that separated workers from managers, which workers quietly resented but felt they could not challenge.

Despite investing considerable time and energy in developing the 'Company Principles', their practical impact upon relations between managers and workers was limited. Tensions arose, in part, from management's efforts to encourage workers to take greater responsibility for the success of the business whilst at the same time itself making unilateral decisions which directed effort in order to improve efficiency. Sometimes this resulted in direct intensification of effort at the expense of workers' good will. Moreover, managers differed in their practical interpretation of the 'Company Principles'. Some senior managers even continued to believe that a traditional punitive approach to discipline was of value, suggesting that the cultural transformation of management was incomplete.

Whilst one might expect to find differences of approach between individual managers in any situation, at the chocolate works the power which individual line managers could exercise over individual workers was unmediated and considerable. As one might expect, workers held a broad spectrum of views about their line managers. Those who showed their appreciation of good work, listened to workers' points of view, and could share a laugh and a joke were judged as 'good blokes'. Judgements about individual managers aside, however, workers understood that the system allowed managers to develop different approaches and to exercise considerable discretion. Underpinning their perception of all managers, was the belief that they were men of great influence and authority, who exercised considerable say over their individual prospects. These factors contributed to workers' rather conservative embrace of the new culture. Most managers knew that workers, especially those with long service, expected them to take the tough approach to discipline. Managers judged that although the company's industrial relations policies were highly progressive, most workers still regarded them with an element of fear. Whilst such fear served management ends, it also inhibited the development of the positive working relationship enshrined within the 'Company Principles'.

For the most part, workers felt that they had little choice but to comply with management requests, making pragmatic acceptance of the authority which managers could command over their individual circumstances. They were able to do so, in part, because the 'hazard' posed to individuals by such concentration of power was generally unrealised for most workers. The company's indirect approach to supervision ensured that many workers met their manager relatively infrequently. And whilst some ambitious workers sought to bring themselves to their manager's attention, others who were less ambitious could generally avoid it. The small number of individuals who were caught and disciplined occupied a marginal position within the workforce, and tended to be regarded simply as 'unfortunate'. Breaking the rules brought the prospect of tough discipline, but the chances of being caught were often low. Managers' disfavour and the label of a 'bad attitude' were generally acquired only after transgressions in the company's most traditional aspects of discipline:

You can do just about anything you like here, as long as you aren't absent or late! (Worker)

Some line managers agreed. Although they made an annual appraisal of each worker in their charge, they found it hard to provide detailed comment on most workers' performance:

At the appraisals you only pick up the very good and the very bad. To the ones in the middle you only ever say 'hello'. Most below-standard appraisals are for absence and bad timekeeping. (Line manager)

In practice, therefore, the company's traditional approach to discipline still formed an important element within the workers' view of their relationship with the company. Management's prerogative rested largely upon older established understandings about its right to discipline workers. Within these understandings it was, to a large degree, accepted that management did not always take place on the basis of workers' agreement. This is borne out below in examining workers' attitudes towards the company's approach to consultation and communication.

Consultation and communication

The company's distinctive approach to management, and the suggestion that a line manager should 'represent the company to the people and his people's views to the company' was reflected in its approach to employee involvement.

'Job involvement' meetings, or 'JI's' were held on each shift, about once every two months, and were convened by management. Line managers briefed workers on company performance, or changes in company employee relations policy, and answered workers' questions about various matters. Sometimes managers made elaborate presentations specially prepared by senior management or by the personnel department. On other occasions they spoke to their own brief. After each meeting managers were obliged to submit a written account of the meeting to the personnel department and to senior management, including a record of issues raised by workers, and an account of the explanation they had provided. In short, the system was designed to provide senior management with a formal means of uncovering the mood on the shop floor. Workers were not obliged to attend the meetings but, as far as was evident, the majority of them generally did so.

Managers believed that the meetings provided workers with a clear opportunity to express their feelings about decisions. They also believed that the meetings often provided them with a clear feel for shop floor views. In some of the meetings attended during the study, workers did make criticisms of the way the company was managed, and blamed senior management for the way in which poor performance was adversely affecting their bonuses. But most workers believed that job involvement meetings were for one-way management communications rather than for two-way consultation about possible changes. One of them recalled,

he [the manager] said to us at the start of the meeting, 'Right, we've got a lot to get through so I don't want to waste time on questions today'. (Worker)

Another joked,

they're not JI's, they're GI's – group instruction! (Worker)

The shop floor generally believed that even if they did express their views they would have little effect upon decisions. Some believed there was little point in even trying where it risked upsetting relations with their line manager. One worker expressed his feelings thus:

I don't want to say anything bad about this company. Its a good company ... I haven't got long to go and I don't want any trouble. Once at a JI I spoke my mind to the manager. Two weeks later I found myself being transferred to another job and I reckon that speaking out cost me £50 a week in wages that I could have earned. Some managers are alright, but others you've got to watch. (Worker)

This worker believed that his manager had given him a less favourable job because he judged him to have a 'bad attitude'. The importance which some workers placed upon maintaining good personal relations with their line manager therefore discouraged them from expressing their own point of view.

In partial recognition of the difficulties which might result from managers acting as the principal means of representation, the company appointed a long serving worker on each shift to improve communications. Part of their duties were to 'pick up the vibrations' from the shop floor, providing an account to their manager of shop floor feelings on particular issues or problems. Additionally these workers gave their colleagues advice about how to tackle problems, explaining company policies, and arranging appointments between individual employees and personnel managers. In practice, however, it was difficult to understand the activities of shift personnel workers. They did not generally act as a representative if a worker found himself in dispute with the company. Managers varied in their opinions about them. Some said they acted as a reliable barometer of shop floor opinion but others suggested that they simply performed routine administration for the personnel department. Few workers expressed confidence in the shift personnel worker as a means of advice and support:

If I had a problem I'd prefer to go to the manager. At least he might be able to do something whereas the shift personnel operator can't. (Worker)

Moreover the effectiveness with which the shift personnel did 'pick up the vibrations' is doubtful. Fewer than one quarter of workers said that they

Table 5.2 *How often do you speak to the shift personnel worker about*
work, wages and conditions?

row % of respondents in each grade

	very often	fairly often	not very often	never
Grade 1	3	20	33	44
Grade 2	5	13	45	37

N = 145

Table 5.3 *How often do you think your views are taken into account when*
decisions are taken?

row % of respondents in each grade

	very often	fairly often	not very often	never
Grade 1	5	22	32	41
Grade 2	5	13	47	35

N = 145

spoke to them on a regular basis and around two fifths never spoke to them
at all (see table 5.2).

The company's practical difficulties in developing employee involvement
stemmed from its longstanding unwillingness to establish independent
employee representation. Workers were generally unable to see managers
as representatives of their interests. Their own experiences made them
aware that managers exercised considerable power in pursuit of goals
which did not always coincide with their own, and indeed might sometimes
be at their own individual expense. Shift personnel operators lacked the
independent authority necessary to represent workers' views to management. In these circumstances, workers felt considerable pressures to defer
to management, and sensed that individual expressions of dissent were
unwelcome. Their feeling that workers had little ability to influence
company decisions was widespread (see table 5.3).

Without independent representation workers lacked the means to
construct a dialogue with management in their own terms, an unusual state
of affairs in a large, mature industrial organisation employing a large
number of manual workers. Factors explaining the absence of a union at

the chocolate works were difficult to uncover. The issue was something of a taboo on the shop floor. Workers told stories of how 'troublemakers' had been eased out through repeated job and shift changes. Many seemed to regard it as an implicit condition of employment that they did not express a desire to join a union:

We've been told that this place would close if there was a union ... a bloke tried to start one once, but he got the sack ... several blokes tried to start one a few years ago, but the company paid them money to leave ... what do we need a trade union here for anyway, our wages are good, it couldn't achieve anything, we're better off without one. (Several workers)

In all probability, workers did not seek to establish independent representation because they believed that their wage premium was paid in lieu of such arrangements. Equally, however, their acceptance of such a situation suggests that the sense in which workers participated in company activities was narrow. They did their jobs with the flexibility which management asked of them, but their motivation for doing so was founded not upon a shared moral code or the 'Company Principles', but upon calculation of the material benefits which they would receive.

Despite introducing 'the Principles', 'job involvement meetings' and 'shift personnel workers', management was not successful in persuading workers that it listened to their views and took account of them in making decisions. Further evidence of the way in which workers thought about their relationship with the company is revealed by examining the new approach to pay and grading.

The payments system and pay

Management introduced a new common approach to pay and grading in order to promote common commitment to a common purpose. The grading scheme provided for around 20 different shop floor grades through which workers could ascend by attending training courses and learning new skills. In practice, however, the 'pay-for-knowledge' system encouraged some workers to identify closely with managers but encouraged less positive attitudes in others.

These difficulties arose from the uneven distribution of opportunities for further training and associated higher earnings. For most grade 2s the prospect of promotion provided a clear incentive. Three fifths (59 percent) of them believed that it was 'very probable' or 'fairly probable' that they would receive some kind of promotion within the next few years. But far fewer grade 1 workers believed that promotion might come their way. In fact, as many as two thirds (67 percent) of grade 1 workers believed that their promotion was improbable. Furthermore, many of them clearly felt that to be denied the opportunity of promotion on account of their failure to pass the necessary aptitude tests was unfair. Over two thirds (70 percent) of shop floor workers, did not believe that the tests took full account of people's work abilities. With such a view being widespread amongst the workforce, workers who were unsuccessful in the tests were less inclined to look upon promotion as the consequence of merit, and more inclined to think that changes in the company's employee relations policies were to their disadvantage and unfair.

The 'pay-for-knowledge' approach worked against some aspects of the new culture which management sought to develop on the shop floor. For example, in the wrapping room, many of the machine engineers were ambitious. Some of them had been recently recruited by the company on the promise of a bright future in return for their hard work. They took the view that much depended upon the way in which their manager looked upon 'their attitude' or, to adopt a catch-phrase often used by the line managers, machine engineers believed that their promotion depended on their demonstrating that they could 'make things happen'. When a manager left the department for any length of time, he would generally ask one of the machine engineers to assume responsibility for production until his return and entrusted him with his telephone paging device, otherwise known as the 'bleep'. Some machine engineers competed for possession of the 'bleep' and drove their colleagues hard in their manager's absence. Such competition turned the 'bleep' into a status symbol which was at odds with management's attempts to build a single status workplace.

It also had other adverse consequences for relationships between workers:

The grade 2s feel they have to get on. Some of them come up here shouting and swearing. Either the sweets are no good or they're waiting for them and they tell us to get a bloody move on. They feel if the manager sees them they'll get promoted. I had a real row with one of them the other day. (Worker)

By proving that they could 'make a contribution', by working hard and accepting an increasingly wider range of tasks, machine engineers had something to gain by developing a positive relationship with their manager. For other workers not eligible for promotion, however, the enthusiasm of certain machine engineers meant more exertion for a much less obvious reward. Such differences of view were at least partly responsible for the arguments that developed between packers and machine engineers over packing speeds. Furthermore, they may well have been influential in management's resort to a traditional style of discipline. Whilst positive approaches to discipline were effective amongst workers who believed they

Table 5.4 *Of all the firms you have worked for, how does this one rate as far as wages (including shift and overtime payments) are concerned?*

row % of respondents in each grade

	the best	above average	below average	the worst
Grade 1	19	66	11	4
Grade 2	30	67	4	0

N = 145

Table 5.5 *How secure do you think your employment is at the works during the next five years?*

row % of respondents in each grade

	very secure	fairly secure	not very secure	not at all secure
Grade 1	20	57	15	8
Grade 2	20	60	17	4

N = 145

had prospects, they were not judged so effective against those workers who thought otherwise. The new approach to pay and grading did not unite workers in common effort, but instead created a situation in which the availability of incentives to some workers was to the detriment of good relations, and to the practice of other company policies, on the shop floor.

Workers' reactions to the new payments system revealed that their attitude towards the company had changed rather less than management hoped for. They continued to think of their relationship with the company overwhelmingly in the traditional terms of 'a fair day's work for a fair day's pay'. This was clearly demonstrated in their reaction to the company's attempt to tie wage increases to improvements in company performance. This rule had been in force for several years and had always resulted in wage increases well in excess of the cost of living. But whilst it was still true that workers judged that wages and job security at the chocolate works were better than generally available elsewhere (see tables 5.4 and 5.5), during the course of this study this apparently positive view of the wage-effort bargain began to change. The substantial and increasing demands made upon workers led them to believe that whilst the company paid better than others, it now asked for disproportionately greater effort. Despite premium wages workers believed that their wage–effort bargain was no longer fair.

Difficulties arose because senior management had set rather ambitious performance targets that year, and when they could not be met declined at first to pay out any bonuses. This caused a good deal of annoyance on the shop floor. Workers felt that despite the fact that they had worked harder than before, management's unrealistic targets had unfairly denied them their just reward. Some seized upon the situation to argue that, 'we haven't had a proper pay rise for years', clearly unimpressed by the company's unwillingness to recognise increases in their cost of living. In remarks like 'all the time more work and no extra money', workers suggested that their wage–effort bargain was no longer so favourable and hinted at declining goodwill.

Things came to a head when management wanted to change the system of shift payments. It wanted to move from the system whereby each shift was paid at a different premium, reflecting social inconvenience, towards a situation where all shifts were paid at the same rate. From management's point of view the new system was both simpler and was the first step in securing greater flexibility in working time. In the usual fashion, line managers held job involvement meetings to explain the changes, and went to some lengths to explain that only a few, if any, workers would lose money. Workers' reactions were, however, unexpected. They expressed their opposition to change with unprecedented force, openly arguing against management proposals:

I don't care what they say, our Sunday afternoons are worth more than our Monday mornings. (Worker)

The line managers were taken aback by the strength of shop floor feeling. One of them mused afterwards,

I think we have gone too far this time. (Line manager)

The company postponed the introduction of the changes. It was an uncharacteristic course of action. Shortly afterwards, the senior management decided to break with the principle of paying wage increases only after performance targets had been reached, and gave all the workers an across the board pay rise. It also altered the bonus scheme to ensure that a similar situation could not arise again.

Workers' reactions to the payments system revealed that they conceived their relationship with the company in traditional terms. The idea of a wage–effort bargain, once the foundation of the company's approach to industrial relations, continued to play an important part in their thinking.

Attempts to link pay to workers' individual performance through the new grading scheme had uneven effects upon motivation, and undermined workers' belief that their wage–effort bargain was constructed upon fair terms. Attempts to make wage increases depend upon improvements in sales performance also impaired morale because workers rejected the principle that they might supply extra effort without due reward. Recognising that co-operation was dependent upon its reputation for paying good wages, the company acted quickly to ensure that its policies on pay reflected workers' attitudes more closely.

Conclusions

The changes which took place in management policies at the chocolate works reflected new and sophisticated thinking about industrial relations. For many years the company's approach to labour relations comprised high standards of effort in return for premium rates of pay. But as management sought greater commitment from workers, an environment in which there was close and autocratic supervision of work gave way to attempts to build a culture in which individuals felt responsible for contributing to the success of the wider organisation.

The company developed a 'philosophy' whose purpose was to bind managers and workers together in the pursuit of common goals. Individual employees were encouraged to take responsibility for improvements in efficiency and quality. Symbols of status and authority were eliminated because management believed that they created barriers within the productive community, inhibiting co-operation. The company implemented a new payments system which rewarded all employees according to common principles reflecting their responsibilities, and which linked wage increases to company performance. On the shop floor, supervision was eliminated as workers were organised into autonomous groups. Managers were committed to encouraging their subordinates to accept wider responsibilities; they generally took a long term view when things went wrong, adopting positive rather than punitive approaches to discipline, in the belief that it would encourage workers to take greater responsibility for decision-making in future.

Yet despite management's careful planning, it proved difficult in practice to reconcile the various goals of the 'Company Principles'; there were tensions between management's ambition to improve continuously the efficiency of the business and its belief that such activities were best devolved to production workers. The discretion accorded to line managers allowed differences of approach to develop. Some managers chose to run their shifts by economising on labour, pushing their workers hard, sometimes to the point where they responded by restricting their effort. Management's faith in the new culture was also easily shaken. Alongside the positive approach to discipline, it sometimes resorted to more coercive measures, outwith the spirit of a joint approach and more in keeping with the traditional style of rule-making at the works. The 'first and last hour rule' was a 'decree' intended to enforce standards set by management. It signified to the shop floor not a shared sense of purpose but rather the continuation of a punitive management style. Whilst this rule secured improved standards of discipline, it did so at the expense of goodwill. Despite the care and effort that the company expended in the development of the 'philosophy', it served as only a partial guide to management's behaviour on the shop floor.

Beneath the extensive changes that took place in industrial relations policies, other more fundamental aspects of management style remained unaltered. Committed to continuing unitarism, albeit of a sophisticated kind, there were limited opportunities for workers to participate other than in suggesting ways directly to improve company performance. It is true that some authors have visited non-union workplaces and spoken positively about the quality of worker participation in decision-making. For example, Cressey *et al.* (1985) sketched a picture of 'Comco' in which a policy of common status for all employees contributed to an environment of flexible, informal work routines, in which authority relations were transformed into 'dialogues' founded upon some kind of 'social contract' (p.41). In such an environment, 'participation ... permeated working and social relation-ships' to create genuine mutual commitment to the aims of the enterprise. In view, however, of their observations about the comprehensiveness of management prerogatives (p.44), and the importance which workers attached to the rewards package (p.51), it would be easy to read too much into these remarks. Beneath the apparent informality of single status work relations at the chocolate works, workers did not feel involved in decision-making. In many instances, relations between individuals and their managers were not developed beyond occasional conversations in which subordinates showed due deference and a 'positive attitude'. The extent to which managers could influence an individual's prospects inhibited some workers from expressing disagreement with management decisions, either personally or at job involvement meetings. Without independent means of representation, workers found it difficult to make representations of their interests to management. Management's communications policies gener-ated pressures to conform rather than commitment.

Workers' reactions to management plans were generally conservative. They continued to believe that their interests were separate from and different to those of the company. Having for many years been encouraged to think of their employment as a wage–effort bargain, they often looked upon line managers' activities simply as a means of increasing the burdens placed upon them. Whilst a great majority of the workforce felt that their jobs were both well paid and secure, many workers also tended towards the view that management was stretching existing understandings beyond reasonable limits. The 'pay-for-knowledge' system cut against their ideas of 'fairness', and they judged that the scheme for linking pay to company performance was eroding the value of their wage premium. Eventually, management was obliged to modify the principle of performance-related pay and, in response to mounting discontent, concede an across the board increase related to the cost of living.

The evidence presented in this study therefore suggests that it is difficult to make sophisticated unitarism work in practice. It proved difficult to reconcile the goals of management and workers in a company philosophy. The pressures resulting from the drive for continuous improvement could not be resolved within management's fundamental attachment to unitarism and workers' narrow view of their employment relation, except through increases in wages. Beneath the apparent sophistication of management techniques, the workers' relationship with the company was narrow, based not upon an extended sense of commitment but upon the limited obligations implicit in a wage–effort bargain.

More broadly it suggests that even sophisticated non-union firms, perhaps still relatively few in number but often portrayed as the trailblazers of the new human resource management, do not find it easy to make these approaches work well. This study, like the small number of others in similar environments (see, for example, Geary 1992a, 1992b), has found that despite considerable management effort to create a more broadly based relationship between workers and the company, many aspects of the old industrial relations inevitably seem to coexist alongside the new. A closer look at the way in which new techniques work in practice must also cast doubt upon the idea that sophisticated non-union employers have found an intrinsically better way to manage employees. At the chocolate works management policies sometimes encouraged workers in excesses of individualism which cut against the development of common commitment to a common purpose. In other instances, as in workers' reaction to the profit-related pay scheme, there is evidence that positive effects upon motivation were counterbalanced by a demotivating effect.

Evidence of tensions on the non-union shop floor all too often resulted from lack of effective means by which workers could make representation of their views to management. Without any clear mechanisms for this purpose, not only was management unable to take full account of shop floor views, but it was also unable to convince workers that the introduction of human resource management policies was subject to widespread agreement. This served to diminish their effectiveness. Ultimately, as both this study and others have illustrated, it seems that the motivation of workers in sophisticated non-union firms may still rely to a considerable degree upon their knowing that their wages are higher than those paid by alternative employers. For this reason, one may doubt whether sophisticated unitarism, as currently practised, is really a generalisable model for industrial relations.

Chapter 6 draws together evidence from the previous chapters, and considers what light they can throw upon the way in which new developments in industrial relations have taken place. What difficulties have management faced in introducing change necessary to meet the challenges of competition? What are the prospects of securing genuine co-operation on the shop floor?

6   Willing Slaves?

Introduction

There can be little doubt that British industrial relations have changed in recent years. Two distinct attempts to explain the course of recent developments were sketched in chapter 1. The first, traditional in orientation, suggested that the recent absence of overt industrial conflict might have been little more than a temporary phenomenon, a reaction to unfavourable external conditions in which managers and workers had created an 'alliance of insiders'. Moreover, according to this view, co-operation between managers and workers has rarely extended beyond the barest minimum necessary to avoid enterprises being bankrupted by the forces of competition. In short, beneath a thin veneer of industrial peace, managers and workers have continued to regard each other as adversaries. The second, alternative point of view, argued the possibility that innovations in management policy may have given rise to the development of a 'new industrial relations', in which managers and workers have learned to co-operate in the pursuit of common goals. In this more optimistic account, adversarial attitudes have been displaced by a constructive approach based upon joint problem-solving.

Beneath their obvious differences, however, the traditional and the 'new industrial relations' accounts share certain ideas about how and why the world has changed. Indeed, it is their common assumptions which provide the starting point for a broader understanding of contemporary developments. Both accounts reflect the belief that market forces have become increasingly powerful, and now constitute the most important influence upon workplace behaviour. Enhanced competition within product markets has exercised influence over managers, whilst related changes in labour markets have been experienced by workers. This distinctive emphasis is worthy of further exploration. Amongst the most interesting findings of previous workplace studies was not only the idea that market pressures were just one amongst other influences upon shop floor relations, but also the view that they were less than straightforward in their effects. Drawing upon the evidence of the preceding chapters, this chapter considers how, and to what degree, product and labour market pressures may have influenced managers and workers respectively. It contemplates also, their relative importance and interaction with other features of life on the shop floor in preventing and promoting change.

There are further similarities between the traditional and 'new industrial relations' accounts. Both suggest that in recent years management has adopted a more 'unitarist' view of organisational life, in which there is less scope for organised opposition to management plans. Both argue that management has been successful in realising this view, achieving a greater degree of control over work, and that workers have acquiesced rather than opposed change. In this chapter such propositions are re-evaluated by comparing evidence from the preceding case studies. Have managers been able to extend their control over work? Have changes in industrial relations reflected a narrower basis of agreement between managers and workers than in the past, or have they been founded upon successful new mechanisms for integrating the interests of companies and employees? The extent to which workers have been able to influence change is also considered alongside suggestions that their attitudes towards work may have changed. Finally this chapter explores why co-operation has arisen in some workplaces rather than others, and reflects upon whether contemporary management initiatives have laid the basis for more co-operative industrial relations in the future.

Managers

New ideas and practice

A number of recent accounts suggest that managers have responded to growing international competition by refashioning industrial relations around a clear organisational purpose (Kochan *et al.* 1986; Storey 1989). There were echoes of this in all three of our case studies. In each one, managers identified intensified international competition as the spur to their attempts to improve efficiency, and in some circumstances they had even come to believe that an organisation should serve a single goal. Thus management at the chocolate works deliberately avoided establishing an elected Works Council because it believed that such a body might establish priorities at odds with management goals. Similarly at the frozen food works, management no longer intended to approach shop floor workers on matters of work organisation via their elected shop stewards. This 'cultural imperative' was not universally appreciated, however. At the biscuit works, despite the general view that competition had increased, managers remained committed to pluralism. Here, senior managers continued in the firm belief that preserving and extending their control was compatible with the existence of formally independent, representative workplace institutions. They preferred to raise standards within the terms of a customary joint approach to industrial relations, preserving the importance of shop stewards, and achieving substantial flexibility through skilful management of the 'culture of politeness' which had been developed over many years.

These differences suggest that the recent appeal of unitarism is likely to have been in part a reaction to managers' experience of the past, and in part a reflection of the way they have identified solutions to organisational problems. At the chocolate works organisational pluralism had never become an established part of management thinking, and individual managers had never encountered organised worker opposition to their plans. Managers identified their 'industrial relations problem' as improving workers' motivation, and the solution as making better use of their talents. But at the frozen food works, managers turned towards the 'new industrial relations' because they believed that their existing approach, founded upon pluralism, had failed to deliver even the most minimal degree of co-operation. They looked towards unitarism as a means of fundamentally reconstituting employees' perceptions of their obligations to the company, of moving from adversarial to non-adversarial industrial relations. It may be the case, therefore, that if the experiences and judgements of managers in these case studies are anything to go by, the appeal of the 'new industrial relations' and its unitarist underpinning may have been greatest either where unitarism has historically formed a part of management's approach, or where it has offered the prospect of transforming existing fortunes.

Existing accounts have tended to characterise managers' practical expression of their belief in unitarism in either of two ways. On the one hand, traditional accounts have suggested that managers have become more confident in asserting their 'right' to manage, advocating an 'unsophisticated unitarism'. On the other, the 'new industrial relations' has pointed to a new kind of 'sophisticated unitarism' in which managers have convinced workers that they share similar interests. Evidence from the chocolate works and the frozen food works, however, suggests that such a distinction is difficult to maintain. In practice, management views turned out to be a complicated mixture of both sophisticated and unsophisticated approaches.

Senior managers at both the chocolate works and the frozen food works believed that improving workers' commitment to the company purpose was an integral part of the adoption of broader aspects of the new management ideas. They argued in favour of a sophisticated ideal in which modern methods of production and quality control required that shop floor workers be trained across a wider range of jobs and accorded greater discretion in performing their tasks. By encouraging workers to learn a wider range of jobs, managers hoped that a virtuous process of improvement would begin. They believed that as workers were given the opportunity to participate in assuring high standards of quality, so both results and morale would improve. In short, managers judged that greater worker commitment to company goals was an integral part of the successful adoption of more efficient methods of production.

Yet even where managers were keen to introduce the 'new industrial relations', their commitment to innovative approaches co-existed with a desire to preserve conventional aspects of management authority. Management at both the chocolate works and the frozen food works retained conventional approaches to discipline. At the chocolate works, management continued to regard good timekeeping as the basis of 'high standards', retaining both the practice of clocking and a substantial 'good timekeeping bonus'. Furthermore, it continued the practice of disciplinary 'decrees' prohibiting certain kinds of behaviour on pain of costly penalties. At the frozen food works, managers retained 'Work or want'. Twenty years of combatting the continuous development of restrictive practices inclined them to believe that they required a coercive weapon in the future, despite the failure of such tactics in the past.

The evidence of our case studies, like much other evidence from Britain and elsewhere (see, for example, Hendry *et al.* 1988), suggests that managers in general may have been driven by increased competition in the product market to improve efficiency and alter their approach to industrial relations. But the changes which have been introduced may have reflected an understanding of organisational problems which has itself often been influenced by the existing culture of an organisation. Where managers have judged that pluralism has failed or have found it ideologically unacceptable, they may have embraced 'sophisticated unitarism' with the aim of uniting management and workforce in a common commitment to a common purpose. But at the same time as they have sought to persuade workers of their mission, they may also have attempted to exercise control over work by more customary means. On the basis of the evidence presented in this study, alongside the ideal of 'sophisticated unitarism' lies a practical commitment to less sophisticated unitarist beliefs.

These findings suggest that managers' attitudes and behaviour cannot be easily understood within either of the two accounts of contemporary industrial relations identified in chapter 1. They have sought neither to build an 'alliance of insiders' which was illustrated within the traditional explanation of change, nor have they committed themselves entirely to the 'new industrial relations'. Instead they have attempted to fashion the future in accordance with a complex and idiosyncratic amalgam of old and new ideas. Managers' unwillingness to break with longstanding attitudes, and in some cases their failure to re-evaluate where they went wrong in the past, poses interesting issues. For example, some commentators have argued that the successful implementation of new 'human resource management' techniques depends upon managers in all parts of a business being agreed upon a coherent, philosophical view of the employment relation (see, for example, Hendry and Pettigrew 1986 p.5). Yet in this respect, the evidence reveals differences in the nature of old and new management ideas which are so great as to make one doubt whether management has in practice been able to meet this basic qualification for effective change. Whilst managers saw their function as shaping the organisation to cope with external pressures, they were blind to some of their own existing customs and attitudes. For these reasons, one might conclude, as have others (see, for example, Sisson and Storey 1990), that any cultural transformation of British management has been only partial, and its embrace of the 'new industrial relations' piecemeal.

Workers

Both traditional and 'new industrial relations' accounts of change suggest that workers have accepted new management initiatives. In both explanations, factors external to the workplace have allegedly influenced this acceptance. In the traditional account, market discipline has been by far the most important factor in accounting for change. In the 'new industrial relations' account market forces have created a climate conducive to change, although workers' newly found positive enthusiasm for work has also stemmed in large part from management policies which have improved their 'quality of working life'.

Although each of these explanations has provided an orderly account of workers' behaviour, they have both relied to a surprising degree upon conjecture. There is little empirical evidence about the way in which workers have actually experienced and responded to market discipline. Suggestions that workers have made uncomplicated acceptance of management plans because of their appreciation of the situation in the wider economy have therefore been obliged to assume a great deal. Using evidence from the preceding chapters, however, it is possible to examine how and why workers' behaviour has changed in recent times as a result of pressures which are external to particular workplaces.

External influences

Many commentators have suggested that developments in labour markets have been influential in accounting for a transformation in workers' attitudes towards work. It is possible, for example, that increases in real wages throughout the 1980s may have increased workers' willingness to work. Persistently high levels of unemployment throughout the decade may also have increased the opportunity cost of resistance to management plans. From a traditional point of view, in the context of recent times, workers may have concluded that their wage–effort bargain has not worsened but improved (Terry 1989). And from a 'new industrial relations' point of view, it may be that workers have been encouraged by improvements in real wages to believe that employers are no longer seeking to minimise the wage-bill, and that the idea of a wage–effort bargain is therefore no longer relevant to their employment.

Both traditional and 'new industrial relations' accounts have therefore suggested that where real wages have risen it is likely that workers will have become more amenable to management suggestions for change. Thinking along these lines has perhaps been made all the more plausible because it has fitted well with an oft-asserted connection between two highly visible features of recent industrial relations, namely rising real wages and declining industrial action. Difficulties arise, however, when trying to apply such market-orientated thinking to the situations which arose in each of our case studies.

Table 6.1 shows that at both the chocolate works and the frozen food works, the majority of the workers surveyed tended to believe that they were well paid relative to opportunities elsewhere. But although each group of workers believed they enjoyed favourable relative wages, their behaviour towards management was very different. In one instance, high wages co-existed with workers' muted complaints about high standards of effort required by management, and substantial compliance with managerial prerogative. In the other, workers' perception of a more favourable relationship between wages and effort co-existed with well developed patterns of effort restriction. Such differences suggest that it cannot be taken for granted that favourable wage rates have proved a sure basis of agreement to high standards of effort. Baldamus himself made this point clearly. Although he recognised that relatively high wages can, in limited circumstances, be successful in buying co-operation, 'in the real world the problem is complicated by the fact that effort is also affected by various management controls ... moreover, different types of effort control are used simultaneously' (1957 p.192). In other words, only if everything else had remained constant would it be possible to attribute changes in workers' behaviour to increases in real wages.

The extent to which improvements in real wages have been effective in securing high standards of effort and co-operation is likely to have varied a good deal according to the presence of other factors. Moreover, even where wage rises have been part of a broader attempt to develop the 'new

Table 6.1 *Workers' views upon their wages relative to those paid elsewhere*

row % of respondents

	the best	above average	below average	the worst
Chocolate works	22	66	11	1
Frozen food works	29	31	27	13

Chocolate works: $N = 151$

Frozen food works: $N = 94$

industrial relations' their effect is not likely to have been sufficient to overcome workers' belief that employment is essentially an adversarial relationship. At the chocolate works, workers looked upon their wage premium as payment in lieu of collective bargaining. Although high wages did contribute to making the explicit practice of effort-bargaining irrelevant, it still figured in workers' attitudes and behaviour. At the frozen food works, the tradition of effort bargaining remained an important part of workers' attitudes towards their employer. More generally, these findings suggest that arguments which have laid stress upon favourable wage rates have probably exaggerated the effect of relatively high rates of pay upon workers' behaviour.

Turning from the influence of wages, to what extent can one find support for the view that high levels of unemployment have caused workers to defer to management plans for new working practices (Metcalf 1989b; Ingram 1991)? Unemployment might have influenced workers' behaviour in several ways. First, increases in the national rate of unemployment might have induced a general feeling of fear which caused workers to become more receptive to employer initiatives. In this sense, unemployment may have acted as a genuine external variable upon the situation on the shop floor because it caused workers to adjust their behaviour on account of the situation in the external market. Second, workers might have paid closer attention to the statements or threats issued by employers about inadequate plant performance and the need for improvements in efficiency. Third, workers might have reacted to the threat of unemployment not by co-operating with management, but by attempting to prevent it from reducing the number of job opportunities. In the reverse of the situation put forward by Richardson and Wood (1989), it is possible to envisage a 'perverse' reaction to external influences, whereby workers as 'insiders' have used all

Table 6.2 *How much worry would it cause you if you were to lose your job at this factory?*

row % of respondents	a lot	a fair amount	not much	none at all
Chocolate works	57	29	10	4
Frozen food works	38	43	14	5
Biscuit works	46	23	22	9

Chocolate works: $N = 147$
Frozen food works: $N = 100$
Biscuit works: $N = 180$

their resources in opposition to management in order to prevent themselves becoming 'outsiders'. It is illuminating to consider the possible operation of each of these mechanisms.

The first and simplest connection between unemployment and workers' behaviour can be dispensed with quickly. The evidence of the preceding chapters showed, particularly in the case of the frozen food works, that workers were not always prepared to concede extensions of management prerogative, regardless of the situation in the labour market. The extent to which rising levels of national unemployment acted as an external variable, inducing a general state of compliance in workers, has therefore probably been quite small.

The second possibility, that individual employers have been able to capitalise on the threat of unemployment in order to secure a change in workers' behaviour, must also be in some doubt. It is true that the prospect of unemployment did induce a feeling of deep anxiety amongst workers in each of our case study factories (see table 6.2).

No doubt, this worry had figured in workers' thinking when each of the companies had made job cuts during the previous eighteen months. Reductions in the workforce at the chocolate works had been managed through early retirements, at the biscuit works through voluntary redundancies, and at the frozen food works through a mixture of voluntary and compulsory redundancies. At each of the factories, workers therefore had good reason to believe they risked unemployment. But equally, although conditions may have existed for developing greater co-operation

Table 6.3 *How secure do you think your employment is at this factory over the next five years (all locations)?*

row % of respondents	very secure	fairly secure	not very secure	not at all secure
Chocolate works	31	50	14	5
Frozen food works	12	70	12	6
Biscuit works	6	31	36	27

Chocolate works: $N = 147$
Frozen food works: $N = 100$
Biscuit works: $N = 180$

in both the short run and long run, in practice they lasted only for brief periods. It seems that the conditions for creating an 'alliance of insiders' or a spirit of permanent co-operation evaporated in the months prior to fieldwork because workers quickly re-evaluated their situation.

Table 6.3 shows that despite recent rationalisations, the majority of workers at the frozen food works and the chocolate works made an optimistic evaluation of job security in the medium term. They judged that extensive new investment in the plant made further staff reductions unlikely. Only at the biscuit works did workers feel they were under continued threat of being made unemployed, and they linked this fear specifically to the continuing introduction of new labour-saving production lines. This suggests that it is unlikely that the external threat of unemployment has exercised a direct and lasting effect upon workers' behaviour. Where workers believed that their own employer was about to make redundancies, the fear of unemployment might have provided only short term inducement to an accommodation with management.

Although these findings seem surprising at first sight, they become less so upon reflection. It is not clear that in such circumstances adopting more conciliatory attitudes towards an employer might bring much benefit for workers. Few British employers have felt able to offer their employees the formal commitment of long term employment. In the past they have preferred to shed labour at the earliest opportunity (Williams *et al.* 1989). For workers to grant concessions to their employers over matters in which they have previously been unable to extend trust is only likely to take place in the deepest crisis in which all alternatives are barred (Purcell 1981 pp.236–238). Furthermore, since British workers have always been threatened with job losses, the continuous repetition of the threat may have lessened its impact upon their behaviour. No doubt there have been traumatic circumstances in which such co-operation has been forthcoming, but equally co-operation of this kind may not have easily been sustained beyond the immediate events.

Finally, it is important to consider ways in which workers' behaviour might have diverged from the orthodox market model. If labour market influences operated in an orthodox fashion, this would suggest that where few alternative jobs were available, the costs of unemployment would have been higher, making workers more disposed to develop co-operative attitudes. Once again, however, workers' behaviour did not correspond with this hypothesis. Both the chocolate works and the biscuit works were located in traditionally buoyant labour markets and even during the 1980s the rate of unemployment in their localities was well below the national average. The frozen food works was located within a region in which there were few large industrial employers and where the employment situation had traditionally been more difficult. But contrary to the predictions of the orthodox model the plants in areas of lowest unemployment were those most likely to comply with management plans, whilst the plant in the area of highest unemployment offered considerable resistance. A more plausible, if unorthodox, explanation of workers' behaviour might run as follows.

At the frozen food works, an established combination of relatively high wages and the scarcity of alternative employment may have discouraged quitting and encouraged workers to press disputes within the workplace. In this way, restriction of local job opportunities perhaps served to 'contribute to the growth of militancy among the labour force, the suppression of unorganised conflict giving rise to organised [conflict]' (Hyman 1970 p.178). As a result, rather than quit their jobs for less favourable work elsewhere, a dearth of opportunities beyond the factory may have encouraged workers to stay on the shop floor, using their energies to shape circumstances in ways which ensured their greater protection from market forces, defending existing staffing levels and resisting management attempts to exercise greater control over work. Conversely, in the relatively buoyant labour markets surrounding the chocolate works and the biscuit works, discontented workers traditionally had the option of sacrificing their wage premium in the knowledge that they could pick up a new job elsewhere without too much difficulty. Quitting may have served as a low-cost means of alleviating grievances, and the incentive to develop strong opposition to management may therefore have been correspondingly weaker. Looking at our case studies as a whole suggests that buoyant labour markets may have inhibited the development of strong, independent worker organisation and enabled management to introduce change more easily.

The evidence of wages and unemployment therefore suggests that market forces have not had a uniform or predictable effect upon workers' behaviour. Workers' reaction to the market may often have been parochial and, by the standards of orthodoxy, perverse. It is likely that their behaviour has reflected complex and subtle evaluations of the costs and benefits of particular courses of action, in which the effects of external influences have combined with other factors to result in outcomes which are not easy to predict. Explanations which have relied upon the 'logic' of the external market have therefore probably taken too much for granted. Sustained or long term changes in workplace behaviour are not likely to have arisen solely on account of factors outside the workplace. Understanding change in industrial relations therefore requires one to look inside as well as outside the workplace. As Nolan and Brown (1988) have maintained,

the success with which labour is managed depends less upon the relatively simple task of meeting employees' comparative wage aspirations, than on the endlessly demanding one of creating and maintaining the institutional forms that will maximise their willingness to work efficiently. (Nolan and Brown 1988 pp.353-354)

The following section turns away from considering the external pressures upon industrial relations towards an evaluation of internal influences – the impact of new management policies upon workers' attitudes and behaviour.

Internal influences

New management initiatives in payments systems, job design and management style have longstanding importance in attempts to reform industrial relations. Advocates of the 'new industrial relations' have, like their predecessors in the 'scientific management' and 'human relations' movements, believed that new approaches in these areas have a central role to play in improving workers' moral identification with work.

Payments systems It has long been accepted that managers design payments systems in ways that reflect their beliefs about workers' motivation (Behrend 1959). Similarly, it has long been understood that the ways in which workers respond to payments systems reflect their views about their relations with management (Roy 1955). For these reasons it may be doubly important that in recent years managers have increasingly come to believe that it is no longer necessary to approach the subject of pay in an adversarial way. They have moved away from attempts to motivate workers within the terms of a wage–effort bargain towards the view that managers and workers have a shared interest in achieving better performance (Gregson and Ruffle 1980; IRRR452).

Developments in payments systems at the chocolate works and the frozen food works reflected managers' changing views about workers' motivation much in this way. They sought to reform payments systems in the belief that workers labour most productively under circumstances where their obligations are not narrowly defined by a 'rate for the job', but where they are instead able to take a broader view of their responsibilities. Management at the chocolate works therefore replaced the idea of a 'rate for the job' with a 'pay-for-knowledge' system designed to foster flexibility and a mutual commitment to the allocation of rewards on the basis of merit. Similarly, managers at the frozen food works sought to end once and for all the endless haggling over rates for particular duties by establishing a common rate of pay. In both instances, managers liked to argue that their approach to pay was based upon rewarding flexibility, rather than the performance of specific tasks.

The evidence suggests, however, that workers did not respond to these new ideas with the same enthusiasm as managers. At the chocolate works, where the greatest number of 'new industrial relations' changes were enacted, the 'pay-for-knowledge' scheme failed to bring about significant change in workers' attitudes and did not gain the widespread support of shop floor workers. Although management believed that the system related rewards to individual merit, many workers disagreed. Whilst management wanted to reward those workers who displayed an aptitude for learning skills quickly, many workers thought that merit was better reflected by long service and their own views of what constituted hard work. From their point of view, the criteria which management used to make such judgements about who was most deserving of additional reward discriminated 'unfairly' against many of them.

In each situation the new payments systems did little to reconcile managements' and workers' expectations about rewards and efforts. The expectations gap which arose between them was manifested in their deteriorating relations. At the frozen food works, management control over standards of effort was progressively weakened as shop stewards became suspicious that management intended to cut staff and increase the demands placed upon the remaining workers. Workers responded by adopting restrictive interpretations of the working practices agreement. At the chocolate works, the failure to reconcile management's and workers' expectations of effort and rewards led workers to believe that management had forced a tighter wage-effort bargain upon them. Morale and motivation suffered accordingly, and the problem became so acute that management felt obliged to grant a 'cost of living' pay increase quite at odds with its earlier determination to award pay increases only on the basis of company results.

Despite management's reform of payments systems, workers continued to look upon their employment in conventional terms. When the chocolate workers' profit-related bonus scheme failed to pay out they felt that they should be paid for the effort they had supplied in good faith. Even though the chocolate workers were paid a premium in lieu of collective bargaining, their view of the employment relation therefore involved an implicit wage–effort bargain. Similarly, at the frozen food works the tradition of bargaining was continued on workers' behalf by stewards, who negotiated the terms of their flexible working practices. For example, in the 'bulk box dispute', they preferred to argue that certain kinds of duties were 'outwith the scope of the agreement' rather than concede additional flexibility to management. In both cases the wage–effort bargain remained a deeply embedded feature of workers' attitudes towards employment. Even though managers' ideas about how workers should see their employment relation had changed, workers' beliefs had altered to a much lesser degree.

New initiatives on payments systems failed to bring about a change in workers' attitudes towards their job because management was not successful in generating mutual agreement as to what constituted a 'fair day's work for a fair day's pay' (Lupton 1961; Burawoy 1979; Willman 1982). At the chocolate works management pressed ahead with a 'new industrial relations' payments system without fully consulting the workforce. Its failure to gain workers' agreement to the criteria for 'promotion on merit' generated hostile attitudes towards change. At the frozen food works, management's intention to eliminate longstanding practices of shop floor bargaining worked against trust and created suspicion. Only at the biscuit works did managers motivate workers by gaining their agreement to the wage–effort bargain. They recognised the importance of accommodating workers' views by carefully preserving the rituals of bargaining over the terms of 'favours'. Within a tradition of low basic wages, 'unofficial overtime' payments served as jointly determined incentives to flexible working. Sure enough, there were occasions when this approach failed. These were the instances when workers refused to work overtime as a personal protest against a particular manager or job, or when haggling over the size of 'unofficial overtime' payments could not bring about a mutually acceptable bargain. But these situations were exceptional. Managers at the biscuit works successfully motivated workers because they engaged them in a process which generated mutual agreement about the relationship between effort and reward.

Developments in payments systems at the chocolate works and the frozen food works reflect modern management's increasing desire to foster greater worker commitment to organisation goals. Yet managers' lack of success in these instances might offer a salutary warning to managers elsewhere contemplating change. Conventional attitudes persisted and workers continued to offer limited commitment to employment because new payments systems were not based upon a sufficient measure of mutual agreement. It is true that where there were no formal traditions of effort bargaining management had the freedom to alter the terms of the relationship between reward and effort without workers' prior agreement. But management's freedom was at the expense of workers' morale. Where a strong tradition of effort bargaining was established, management found that in practice workers were unwilling to relinquish their customary jurisdiction. In each case attempts to enforce management initiatives upon workers served only to promote discord. From a broader perspective, new approaches to rewards inspired by new and sophisticated unitarist ideas may not offer the possibility of reconciling managers' and workers' separate expectations of work. Their failure may have been rooted in a tendency to undervalue the importance of seeking motivation through a continuous and mutually-respected process of dialogue.

Job design   Managers have long doubted the effectiveness of scientific management. Instead, they have often preferred to believe that it is possible to improve productivity by altering the nature of jobs in order to provide workers with opportunities for problem-solving and decision-making. The evidence suggests that this belief has grown stronger within the 'new industrial relations', and it is therefore not surprising that it was reflected in the thinking of managers in introducing reform at the chocolate works and the frozen food works. In both instances they moved away from an approach to work organisation based upon scientific management towards a division of labour in which workers performed a broader range of tasks with less formal supervision. Ostensibly, re-designing jobs did not simply involve removing demarcation and reducing staff numbers, it was part of an initiative to transform relations between workers and managers, bringing about looser and more participative relations between colleagues.

Longstanding dissatisfaction with conventional approaches to work organisation has in the past given birth to similarly inspired initiatives. As a rule, their effects have been judged disappointing, either because management commitment to change was superficial and short term, or because its avowed intention to develop looser authority structures was simply a gloss upon deeper difficulties in maintaining control over work (see Berg *et al.* 1978; Friedman 1977, respectively on these points). More recent initiatives may be different from their predecessors. They have been founded upon a body of thought which has allegedly provided a blueprint for integrating improvements in standards of efficiency and quality with enriched social relations. It is also possible that the emergence of these ideas has reflected greater management professionalism and commitment than in the past. This is because they may have been founded upon agreement about priorities which are common to both production and personnel management, rather than one or the other alone (Wilkinson *et al.* 1991). In addition to these factors, new initiatives may have been implemented in conditions of decreasing rather than increasing labour militancy. For these reasons, they are less likely to have been panic measures introduced by management as concessions to organised labour. Instead, modern reform may have offered management an opportunity to integrate labour relations policies with broader long term policies for successfully addressing the challenges of international competition.

The idea that greater efficiency may be achieved by ensuring that high standards of quality are 'built-in' at the moment of production has become a keystone of current management thinking (see, for example, Deming 1970; Juran 1976). The principal emphasis upon developing participative procedures for monitoring and reviewing quality has reflected an attempt to effect deeper cultural change within organisations. As managers have attempted to involve workers in the 'continuous improvement' of production, they have done so in the belief that it can bring a greater degree of openness and trust to their relationships (Bradley and Hill 1983 p.293; Oliver and Davies 1990; Lincoln and Kalleberg 1990). However, for quality, efficiency and good industrial relations to be connected within a 'virtuous circle', managers must have been successful in reconciling looser authority structures with the need to sustain competitive production. On this point, the evidence from our case studies suggests that management has fallen short of its objectives.

Efforts to build a culture of 'continuous improvement' were reflected in new approaches to job design at both the frozen food works and the chocolate works. Workers were formally granted greater responsibility for identifying and resolving production problems. Yet the effectiveness of new ideas and the extent of cultural change in each organisation was limited. It proved difficult to transform the nature of manual jobs. Furthermore, managers were inexperienced in putting the new ideas into practice. They had great difficulty in reconciling the tensions that arose in attempting to sustain quality, efficiency and worker autonomy, the three crucial and interdependent elements of the new approach. These factors inhibited change.

Although the transformation of manual labour may be a pre-condition for closer identification with management, it must also be open to doubt whether, even after substantial reform, manual labour really provides the same opportunities for satisfaction and involvement as managerial and professional work. This doubt arose many times during observation of the shop floor. For much of the time, workers' daily involvement with the issue of quality amounted to little more than the regular performance of prescribed and routine checks which afforded little opportunity to exercise new skills or discretion. In private, some managers at the chocolate works expressed scepticism about the benefits of such changes. For example, one manager noted that although his workers were paid a wage equal to that of many professional workers, they often displayed little enthusiasm for their work. Another explained that 'mass boredom' was the biggest barrier to gaining workers' commitment. At the frozen food works, workers preferred the new work regime because it afforded them greater leisure opportunities. They valued these opportunities more highly than extra effort, which in their view would benefit the company alone. Whatever workers' commitment to their jobs, it existed alongside commitment to other ends. Here, as in other studies, the re-design of manual industrial jobs did not enhance workers' motivation (see, for example, Wall et al. 1986).

Relations between managers and workers encountered difficulties as management was faced with choices about how to reconcile looser authority structures with the need to sustain high levels of production. The new approach did not combine easily with management's continued belief in its right to intervene whenever it felt that it was necessary to increase production. At the chocolate works, when managers decided that 'the needs of the business' required fewer employees on a particular job, or an employee to perform a different job, flexibility was always more important than autonomy. At the frozen food works management prevented work groups taking short cuts for their own ends, creating the impression that the changes in working practices were designed to benefit management alone. Such management interventions had negative consequences for the development of a participative culture.

Workers' commitment to quality initiatives was also impaired because, in their view, it was not matched by a similar commitment from management. For example, when management at the frozen food works relaxed standards in order to raise output, arguments took place between the shop floor and supervisors. Management did not consult the shop floor prior to making this decision, and consequently some workers who had volunteered to become part of the quality checking team asked to be returned to normal duties, refusing to take further part in the initiative. The atmosphere in the weekly briefing meetings between managers and the workforce was awkward and tense. The vegetable workers conspicuously used them to remind supervisors of the limits to their authority, whilst the shop stewards in the meat department went even further, using these sessions to manipulate an agenda of workplace issues. For example, in order to deflect management from discussions about other aspects of work performance they seized upon the ineffectiveness of various pieces of equipment, tying management down in technical discussions. The evidence here, as in other cases, suggests that rather than offering opportunities for managers and workers to join in the cause of 'continuous improvement', quality improvement programmes became a forum for articulating the limited trust which managers and workers placed in one another (Bradley and Hill 1983; Griffen 1988). Where management's commitment to production outstripped its commitment to quality, the effects of 'new-style' quality initiatives were limited and sometimes negative.

These difficulties reflected more fundamental management unease about new approaches to discipline. At both the chocolate works and the frozen food works, the new policies depended upon workers voluntarily exercising their talents on behalf of the employer. In such circumstances breaches of discipline became harder for management to detect and the cause of errors became open to a wider variety of interpretations. But in practice, management was unable to commit itself fully to reliance upon 'self-discipline' at the expense of conventional 'corrective' or 'punitive styles'. Instead, new approaches to discipline existed alongside long established ideas. At the chocolate works, managers imposed punitive sanctions following an incident in which the wrong product recipe was dispensed, taking a view that the process operators had not responded to approaches from the quality checkers informing them that problems were occurring further up the line. Line managers listened to workers' accounts of the situation but made the decision to impose sanctions amongst themselves. They used the 'corrective' approach in a further range of management interventions including the weekly 'housekeeping audit', prompted by the desire to ensure that autonomy did not compromise quality or production standards. Similarly, when the vegetable workers at the frozen food works got into 'bad habits' by spending too long in the canteen and leaving early, management increased the number of supervisors and gave them clear instructions to secure higher standards of effort. The supervisors spent longer periods walking round the shop floor, or watching the production process, attempting to ensure that workers spent longer periods on the shop floor. Success in raising standards of discipline and output was not based upon developing self-discipline through quality improvement groups, but rather through close monitoring of workers' activities. In short, where workers' behaviour did not serve management ends, management soon resorted to more conventional disciplinary measures. Management's willingness to issue direct instructions rather than to allow workers to reach their own decisions may have inhibited the chances of self-discipline developing in the longer term.

Taken together, this evidence suggests that new approaches to work organisation did not succeed in uniting managers and workers in the common cause of 'continuous improvement'. Present advocates of industrial relations reform have, like their predecessors, believed that new approaches to job design are the key to unlocking substantial improvements in standards of job performance and social relations. But in practice the new division of labour did not yield improvements in the intrinsic benefits of manual work and was not accompanied by enhanced worker motivation. Doubts must remain as to whether manual work is capable of being sufficiently transformed to provide scope for high levels of intrinsic satisfaction and motivation. New approaches also proved difficult to implement. Often they were at odds with conventional practices and, as a rule, managers found it hard to place exclusive faith in the ability of a more participative approach to deliver reliable high standards. The consequence was that management behaviour appeared confused because its commitment to expanding workers' autonomy continued to be in competition with its desire to assert broader prerogatives. Although managers may have been talking a new language, their underlying priorities had changed to a lesser degree. The development of trust and self-discipline was therefore correspondingly limited.

Management–worker relations Recent prescriptions for the transformation of industrial relations have stressed that line managers have an important role to play in motivating staff (see, for example, Peters and Waterman 1982; Jackson 1983; Walton 1985; Storey 1988). Common to these accounts has been the idea that effective management should be about creating an environment in which workers feel able to make an appropriate contribution to the benefit of the organisation.

At both the chocolate works and the frozen food works, managers spoke of attempting to cultivate a positive but informal working atmosphere. They wanted to create a new style of management leadership which, in conjunction with their new approaches to job design and rewards systems, could bind the organisation together in a common and unifying purpose. Managers believed that as prescribed routines gave way to opportunities for creative effort, the development of open and friendly relations with workers would play an important role in enabling workers to become committed to company goals.

Changes took place in management structures at both the chocolate works and the frozen food works in an attempt to bring managers into regular contact with their subordinates. Managers wanted to create more 'direct' relationships in which they would personally be able to instil greater motivation and better understanding of company objectives in workers. As in other areas of industry, these problems were believed to have been caused by the previous nature of the relationship between shop floor workers and junior managers or supervisors (Klein 1984). At the chocolate works, senior managers took the radical step of eliminating the supervisory function altogether. Line managers were made the linchpin of the employee development scheme through their responsibility for reporting on each worker's performance once a year. At the frozen food works, management retained supervisors, but in smaller numbers, hoping that they would serve to train workers in a wider and more complex range of skills and decision-making.

Chocolate works At the chocolate works managers made changes not only to management structures but also to symbolic aspects of management authority. Like an increasing number of managers, they believed that constructive management–worker relations could be more effectively developed in situations where managers and workers shared common status (CBI 1981; Mullins 1986; Pegge 1986; Wickens 1988). They talked of the need to eliminate symbols of 'management separateness' and of their intent to do away with 'unnecessary distinctions'. 'Single status' permeated every visible aspect of employment. There was a common car park, canteen, company uniform, and rewards structure. The works director worked within the open plan administration area, through which all workers passed on their way to the production lines. In fact, the management of status at the chocolate works bore substantial resemblance to practices at the electronics factories visited by Cressey *et al.* (1985) and Trevor (1988). In practice, managers and workers spoke to one another on first-name terms, and frequently ate together in the company canteen where they discussed production plans and problems quite openly.

Despite the appearance of an 'open' management structure, however, the underlying reality was rather more complicated. Without the likelihood of organised opposition or potential bargaining, there were positive advantages and few disadvantages in telling workers of company plans well in advance. Although management stressed the importance of each individual worker 'making a contribution' to the success of the business, channels for workers' participation were narrow and to a considerable extent under the exclusive control of management. Despite being required to exercise autonomy during routine production, managers could move individuals at short notice from one job to another without consultation. Changes in workplace rules took place not through consultation but by command.

Single status fashioned the appearance, but had less impact upon the substance of relations between workers and managers.

The management structure played an important part in restricting the ability of managers and workers to construct positive relations. By the admission of both managers and workers, in most instances, the 'direct relationship' existed more in theory than it did in practice. There were too many people on each shift for the manager to know most individuals at all well. For many, annual appraisals tended to concentrate on discussion of 'hard' measures of workers' performance, such as timekeeping and sickness, rather than matters which required managers to have detailed knowledge of workers' strengths and weaknesses. Some workers took the view that avoiding the manager's eye was quite sufficient to ensure adequate relations. Despite the importance which senior management placed upon 'direct relations' between line managers and workers, the nature of the management structure ensured that they tended to remain courteous but distant.

Management's attempts to build a sense of collective commitment to company goals were also inhibited by other labour relations policies which encouraged workers to compete against one another. Machine engineers re-invented their own status symbols by attaching significance to being entrusted with the manager's telephone pager. For these ambitious workers, a good rapport with their line manager, in an atmosphere of informality and first-name terms did not mean the same thing as speaking one's mind; it meant taking opportunities to display one's commitment to company objectives in the hope of achieving promotion. Underneath 'first-name terms' there was a deeper sense of formality. Attempts to encourage individual commitment worked to the detriment of achieving collective commitment.

In short, initiatives to develop a new style of management leadership at the chocolate works embodied a tension between management's commitment to single status and its other practical views about control of the works. Together, these ideas created a management style which marginalised dissent but did not contribute to the development of shared goals.

Frozen food works   After contributing to over twenty years of adversarial relations, managers embarked on a programme of change with mixed feelings. Whilst they sought an end to adversarial relations, many believed that workers would not respond well to the new production arrangements. They regarded a period of poor performance and shop floor indiscipline as proof of their point, and instructed the supervisors to raise standards. Workers and supervisors alike were made more uncertain about what was expected of them. Management's expression of scepticism further confused the situation on the shop floor. Amidst declining production and much less well defined responsibilities for taking corrective action, tensions quickly emerged in acute form. Managers blamed supervisors on the rather inconsistent grounds that they neither enabled workers to reach their own decisions, nor supervised them sufficiently. Workers blamed supervisors for 'interfering', clawing back the concessions they had obtained in negotiating the new working practices agreement. In irritation at having their leisure opportunities restricted, workers expressed their dissatisfaction either by making the supervisors look small or by taking more vigorous action.

At the frozen food works there was rather less change in the symbols and structures of management power than at the chocolate works. Workers and managers shared a single canteen but they rarely sat together at the same tables. On the shop floor supervisors retained their white coats as opposed to overalls, and their distinctive trilby hats. The works retained an identifiable 'culture of separateness' as the new style of management leadership foundered amidst deepening mistrust.

Biscuit works At the biscuit works management introduced relatively little change in the structures and symbols of managers' authority. Management inaugurated a new grade of supervision, but was careful to ensure that the chargehands whose powers were being removed were able to keep every other aspect of their status. Management's apparent commitment to single status went so far as to grant a small number of senior supervisors 'staff status', but co-existed quite amicably with separate management canteens, uniforms with different coloured collars for each grade of shop floor worker, and different benefits provision for staff and non-staff employees. Indeed, although the company had talked about introducing aspects of single status, on the shop floor it seemed keen to preserve a myriad of status differences rather than to eliminate them.

Management and worker relations at the works were characterised by stable understandings about legitimate authority and appropriate responsibilities. The finely divided structure served to 'reduce the distances in outlook and orientation between managers and workers', thereby enhancing social integration at work (Lincoln and Kalleberg 1990 p.254). Within the precise definition of rights and obligations, a mutual commitment to bargaining around the edges of individual responsibilities produced a generally reliable degree of flexibility in order to meet production needs. The good personal relations which characterised their exchanges bore witness to workers' and managers' commitment to bargaining.

A general point about management–worker relations Evidence from the shop floor suggests that personal relations between managers and shop floor workers have changed rather less than one might imagine. Even at the chocolate works, where highly visible policies of single status had been introduced, and workers and managers were brought into regular and direct contact with each other, workers continued to find it difficult to speak their mind to managers, let alone believe that they shared a common interest. Similarly at the frozen food works, although supervisors' duties were modified considerably, the supervisors continued to live an uneasy existence, caught between the demands of management and the pressures from the shop floor. Despite the changes to management structures, and considerable efforts to re-design shop floor jobs, at both the chocolate works and the frozen food works workers' understanding of management prerogative changed little. In contrast, the complexities of hierarchy and bureaucracy which persisted at the biscuit works provided both order and flexibility. Within this complex hierarchy, values of civility, politeness and procedure went some way to reducing tensions and created a sense of dignity and purpose in work. Relations between workers and managers were characterised by their understanding of each other's expectations of work. One might conclude that modern attempts to manipulate workers' perception of status and responsibility have made little progress. Workers' perception of management authority has to date, continued relatively unaltered.

Barriers to change

The foregoing discussion has revealed that neither the 'traditional' account nor the alternative advocacy of a 'new industrial relations' has been able to provide a satisfactory explanation of changes in workplace behaviour. Not only have both of these accounts assumed that managers and workers have been influenced to a uniform and undue degree by the situation in the external labour market, neither has been able to provide an adequate portrayal of behaviour on the shop floor. The 'traditional' view, that managers and workers have continued to look upon their relations in adversarial terms, has proven too restrictive, unable to furnish a satisfactory explanation of management's interest in new approaches to employee relations. For example, at both the chocolate works and the frozen food works major changes took place in management policies for work organisation, rewards, and personal relations between managers and employees. All these measures were directed at overcoming workers' belief that their interests were different from those of their employer. Equally, however, if the traditional account has not allowed sufficient scope for change, the 'new industrial relations' hypothesis has also been proven to be incomplete. Not only has it given inadequate attention to exploring how managers have received and implemented new ideas, assuming their uncomplicated acceptance of the new model, but it has also for the most part neglected any serious exploration of workers' experience of change. The detailed examination of reform presented so far in this chapter suggests that although managers have been experimenting with new approaches to industrial relations, they have not as yet discovered how to make them work on the shop floor. New initiatives in payments systems, job design, and management–worker relations have achieved less than managers hoped for. In short, many managers have headed in the direction of a 'new industrial relations', but the fruits of their endeavours have been more in keeping with conventional approaches.

What might account for this state of affairs? Within the evidence presented here, it is possible to find two broad reasons. First, labour relations in mature plants have been encumbered by their history. This has shaped and coloured both managers' and workers' understanding of new approaches to industrial relations. Second, the 'new industrial relations', as understood and practised by British managers, has been incomplete. Managers have failed to recognise the importance of building a culture of employee involvement through independent representation of workers' views. The particular difficulties which managers have faced in introducing change within mature organisations are elaborated below.

The influence of the past upon the present

When arguing that history worked against commitment, one must also recognise that management played an important role in making that history in the first place. Workplace traditions were, in large measure, the result of past management decisions. In particular, the presence or lack of management success in developing a common company-wide approach to industrial relations policy had a profound effect upon the evolution of workplace co-operation.

Where management had no clear policy, workers fashioned their own distinct and opposing values, strong enough to act as the foundation of powerful challenges to management authority. At the frozen food works management had in the past subordinated all labour relations concerns to other kinds of decisions. As the company's workforce grew rapidly to serve an expanding market for frozen foods during the 1950s, management concentrated upon establishing market dominance rather than a framework for management of industrial relations. In the absence of broad agreement amongst management, a profusion of local arrangements stirred a rising tide of disputes. The practice of independent trades unionism, extensive local bargaining and an adversarial approach to problems became a deep-rooted part of everyday life for everyone at the plant. Once

such behaviour was established, repeated displays of management assertiveness throughout the 1960s and 1970s only served to harden adversarial
views, inhibiting still further the potential for trust to develop.

In contrast, adversarial behaviour did not become part of relationships
at either the biscuit works or the chocolate works. At the former, the
establishment of independent trades unionism was shrewdly forestalled by
management's decision to offer recognition to particular unions of its
choosing, upon terms designed to inhibit adversarial shop floor behaviour.
At the chocolate works management had, since the 1940s, pledged itself to
pay premium wages and benefits which workers in union firms would have
been hard pushed to exceed. Collective representation was forestalled
partly on account of workers' unwillingness to undermine the *raison d'être*
for their wage premium. Both parties entered into a relationship in which
there were distinctive understandings about the extent of management
prerogative and the value of workers' reward. In both the non-adversarial
cases, therefore, management had established a tradition of clear and
consistent views about the conduct of labour relations: at the biscuit works
through a joint approach to rule-making; and at the chocolate works by
paying a premium in lieu of the joint approach.

The cumulative effects of these past management policies towards
industrial relations were the most important influence upon both
managers' and workers' attitudes towards contemporary proposals for
reform. The achievement of a 'new industrial relations' required that they
set aside the beliefs and attitudes of the past, but in practice they found that
doing so was impossible.

Managers found it difficult fundamentally to change their outlook and
behaviour. The legacy of the past was highly influential in their attitudes
towards reform. For managers at the frozen food works devolving
responsibility to the shop floor posed a dilemma. From where they stood, it
seemed that past tendencies to the development of restrictive practices had
been curtailed only through vigorous assertion of their prerogative. Their
unwillingness to withdraw supervision from the shop floor and their
determination to make whatever changes they judged necessary for
development of efficient working practices, reflected their belief that
workers could not be trusted to use their autonomy for company ends.
Similarly, at the chocolate works, the pressure to achieve continuously
good results and high standards tempted managers to issue instructions or
'decrees' in the knowledge that their actions would not be likely to
encounter worker resistance. In both cases managers' customary ability to
secure workers' obedience reduced their incentive to secure workers'
consent or co-operation. The consequence of these dilemmas was that
management policies for reform acquired an air of muddle or confusion.

Even at the chocolate works, where management's approach had in the past exhibited a measure of consistency, new ideas served to complicate the company's approach to employment.

Similarly, workers' reaction to reform proposals was coloured by their experience of management behaviour in the past. Management's vision of the future called upon workers radically to alter their outlook and behaviour. But in the past workers had been discouraged from exercising discretion or autonomy. At the chocolate works, both managers and workers recalled how the environment of strict rules bred substantial obedience, but little in the way of initiative. At the frozen food works, the tough discipline of 'Work or want' was intended to subordinate workers to supervisors' instructions. The legacy of previous management policies was deep-rooted and counter to the new initiatives. This was reflected in workers' behaviour. Conventional attitudes towards rules and shop floor discipline coloured workers' understandings of the 'new industrial relations' in distinctive ways. At the frozen food works, management's past willingness to subordinate labour relations matters to all other aspects of business inhibited the development of workers' trust in management. As misunderstandings arose, workers were predisposed to accept the arguments and leadership of their shop stewards, whose initiative was increasingly exercised against management goals. At the chocolate works, workers continued to be influenced by management's former insistence upon following rules to the letter. They continued to accept strict management directives, but as before covertly maintained their own custom and practice by circumventing managers' instructions so far as this was possible. In each workplace, a legacy of customary management styles continued to permeate workers' understanding of change.

A transformation of the employment relationship proved elusive because it required that managers learn a new way of managing which was at odds with their preceding beliefs about their role. It also relied upon workers exhibiting qualities which they were not previously encouraged to display. It was perhaps not surprising that both parties brought past assumptions with them, for they were their only guide in an otherwise uncertain situation. Managers and workers looked to the past to measure the extent to which they could trust each other in the future. History was against the development of commitment.

The inconsistencies in managements' vision of the future, reinforced workers' conservative reaction to managements' plans. At the chocolate works many workers believed that management's continuing disposition to an authoritarian approach to decision-making posed personal risks to showing initiative. In the adversarial culture of the frozen food works, workers judged that management's goals were still in opposition to their own interests. In each instance, inconsistencies in the management approach led workers to believe that management aims had not changed sufficiently to justify a complete revision of their own attitudes towards employment. At the frozen food works and the chocolate works, where management made substantial attempts to recast the relationship between workers and managers, the changes failed to transform the employment relationship. In neither case had the introduction of policies for a 'new industrial relations' resulted in workers becoming committed to the goals of the enterprise. As a result, many workers continued to look upon employment as a relationship involving limited obligations, although the way in which they expressed this view varied in accordance with their circumstances. In each of these instances, the move to more open management was superficial and, at best, the rapport between managers and workers remained only distant.

According to the evidence of our case studies, although the attitudes of British management towards industrial relations have changed, their new thinking has been muddled and has made only a disappointing impact. As the policies of the 'new industrial relations' have been understood and practised by managers, they have not constituted a successful model for managing employees. The rhetoric of the 'new industrial relations' has outstripped the reality on the shop floor. Influenced by the past, managers have drawn the wrong lessons for the future.

The nature of contemporary reform

Managers' search for a 'new industrial relations' has led them in the direction of an increasingly unitarist approach to reform. Yet the evidence of the studies in this volume suggests that this may not be a stable or productive course in the longer run. Neither at the frozen food works nor at the chocolate works was management successful in gaining workers' commitment to company objectives. For some, this might serve as proof that it is unrealistic to search for such commitment in modern industry (see, for example, Kelly and Kelly 1991). Alternatively, however, it is possible to account for the limits to co-operation in terms of management's failure to secure effective employee involvement in the handling of change.

Management's increasingly visible preference for the unitarist approach has led it away from the belief that formal structures of worker representation can secure high levels of moral involvement in work. Instead managers have placed more faith in policies which relate to workers on an individual basis (Marchington et al. 1992; Findlay 1992). Yet in two respects, the increasing emphasis upon 'direct' at the expense of 'indirect' forms of employee involvement may have generated profoundly adverse consequences for constructive shop floor relations. First, attempts to reduce the influence of elected worker representatives where they have previously been influential may have impaired workers' trust in management. Second, in organisations where there is no provision for elected worker representation in decision-making, decisions made by management alone may attract only limited support from workers. Each of these issues is discussed below.

Although many commentators have argued that trades unions have become universally weak or irrelevant in recent years, the evidence of the preceding chapters suggests that managers ought not to take such a state of affairs for granted. It was certainly apparent that trades unions were unable to exert much influence over broad restructuring decisions like plant closures and redundancies. In the depths of recession when these decisions are more likely to predominate, they create the impression of trades union weakness *vis-à-vis* management. But to argue, as some have, that unions, where they are recognised, must remain permanently emasculated as a consequence of restructuring (see, for example, Terry 1989; Brown 1983), is to underestimate the power which trades unions can still exercise over the organisation of production and other related matters. Whilst it is true that at the frozen food works the union was interested primarily in developments within the local factory rather than in forming relationships with union organisations in the other company plants, this did not render it weak. 'Factory consciousness' was a feature of industrial relations even during periods in which shop floor trades unionism was believed to be strongest (Beynon 1985). Evidence from the frozen food works, alongside other studies (see, for example, Belanger 1985), illustrates that a parochial outlook need not inhibit workers from a vigorous defence of their interests. Whilst management sought to reduce the influence of trades unions, shop stewards were nevertheless able to prevent management from doing so, by developing new tactics which drew directly upon the greater autonomy ceded to workers on the shop floor. Parochial arguments, drawing upon workers' deep-seated distrust in management, enabled shop stewards at the frozen food works to force their way to the centre of management decision-making, frustrating the attempts of managers to bypass them, and foiling their attempts to build a unitarist culture. Sophisticated steward organisation proved surprisingly resilient to the demands made upon it by management's new approach. The shop stewards were successful in blunting management prerogative, restricting effort and raising wages. Commentators have underestimated unions' continued powers of obstruction: even in contemporary circumstances, management may find it counterproductive to bypass a well established workplace union organisation.

Equally, however, management faced difficulties in making the 'new industrial relations' effective in non-union situations. At the chocolate works, management's commitment to unitarism was accompanied by an aversion to representative participation, which led managers towards an uninhibited style of decision-making that resulted in their exceeding the limits of what their subordinates believed to be reasonable or fair. Although the chocolate company's reliance upon high wages was largely successful in containing the development of adversarial behaviour, in the absence of means to persuade workers to co-operate fully with management plans, workers' morale was unstable and declined when their pay prospects deteriorated. Even in non-union establishments, therefore, managers encountered difficulties in creating and sustaining a climate of dialogue and participation amidst other sorts of commercial pressures. The superiority of non-union approaches in raising and sustaining high levels of commitment to a common purpose remains unproven.

The evidence suggests that in organisations, both union and non-union, where management has failed to develop stable means of reconciling managers' and workers' expectations, then the outcome has been at best low or unstable morale. New approaches to industrial relations in both union and non-union firms alike have faced the problem of creating the necessary moral authority for constructive workplace relations. It is perhaps ironic that generating a stable basis for such authority was taken more seriously by the 'old industrial relations' than by new unitarist ideas. The evidence presented in this study illustrates that trades unions were not in themselves the barrier to high morale. Indeed, as many others have argued, it was only where management had deliberately set out to make an element of representative participation an important part of its approach to labour relations that there was a process whereby the company could successfully legitimate change and diffuse local grievances (see, for example, McCarthy and Ellis 1973; Fox and Flanders 1975; Purcell 1979; Thurley and Wood 1983). Management's success at the biscuit works stemmed from the way in which it minimised the unions' power of obstruction whilst at the same time creating opportunities for co-operation. The highly centralised approach to collective bargaining endorsed the company's right to make changes, whilst at the same time creating favourable conditions for the 'culture of politeness'. Management's commitment to collective bargaining posed few obstacles to its plans in practice, but generated the necessary moral authority to ensure orderly and constructive industrial relations. The role of trades unions in the management of change was a measure of the imagination with which management incorporated them within its plans for the future. Trades unions provided a means whereby workers could become involved in decision-making about what constituted 'fair' and 'reasonable' conditions of work. Channels of worker representation played an important part in sustaining workers' morale.

Conclusions

The purpose of this book has been twofold. On the one hand it has examined the adequacy of current explanations of contemporary developments in industrial relations. On the other it has provided its own distinctive account of the way in which workplace relations may have changed.

Current explanations of change, illustrated and compared in chapter 1, have been found wanting. It is not possible to sustain either the traditional account or the 'new industrial relations' thesis. Both explanations for the way in which industrial relations have changed in the past decade have focused upon the way in which external factors have exerted pressure upon managers and workers. Their emphasis upon the effect of product and labour markets has been at the expense of understanding the way in which factors internal to organisations have prevented or promoted change. For this reason both the traditional and 'new industrial relations' explanations of change have been uncritical of the way in which management has implemented its plans, and uncritical in the belief that workers have simply accepted new management initiatives.

To redress the imbalance of existing accounts, this book has examined the detail of workplace behaviour which has occurred in the context of the contemporary reform of industrial relations. An ethnographic approach to studying management–worker relations, set out in chapter 2, afforded the scope to illustrate and begin to explain the complexity of social change to a degree not possible with other research techniques. It provided an opportunity to study developments as they are reflected in the daily routines of the shop floor, penetrating the rhetoric which often accompanies the introduction of new policies, in order to understand change in terms of the cultural perspectives of the parties involved.

The evidence from our case studies shows the different ways in which managers, driven by pressures from the product market, have sought to improve efficiency and the quality of finished goods by thinking afresh about employee relations. The ideal of 'sophisticated unitarism', implicit in their interpretation of the 'new industrial relations', was far removed from the authoritarian suppression of opposition associated with unitarists of bygone days. Instead managers made attempts to cultivate a style of decision-making aimed at encouraging workers to become committed to corporate goals, and provided workers with opportunities to use their talents and energies to serve corporate ends.

Yet it proved difficult to introduce the 'new industrial relations' to mature organisations. Managers' ability to persuade workers of the case for reform was impaired by conflicting pressures and difficult choices, many of which had their roots in the way organisations had historically been managed. Market pressures may have influenced the thinking and priorities of managers to a degree, but they had a much less pronounced effect upon workers. Instead, workers evaluated new management initiatives by relying upon their direct shop floor experience, and by taking account of the situation which had prevailed in the past. In practice it proved difficult to transform manual jobs so that they offered the same degree of intrinsic interest as professional work. Boredom inhibited enthusiasm.

The difficulties that arose in the course of change were particularly visible in organisations which had previously functioned in an adversarial way. Here, the application of 'new industrial relations' techniques failed to produce a transformation because they were unable to resolve the continuing tensions between re-organising production whilst simultaneously developing high levels of trust. Where workers felt strong allegiance to an independent trades union, attempts to reduce its influence were interpreted as a sign of bad faith and contributed to the continuation of adversarial relations. Equally, however, managing without trades unions did not, in itself, prove the key to a harmonious and efficient workplace. Inefficient working practices persisted in the non-union environment as workers economised on effort when the manager was out of sight. Insofar as the non-union environment did prove more responsive to change, workers extended flexibility to management because they believed that their benefits exceeded those likely under collective bargaining. Management obtained flexibility because the firm in question successfully portrayed itself to workers as an exception. This non-union model may not therefore be widely replicated and managing without unions is in itself unlikely to improve workers' commitment.

Even though managers spoke about developing an organisation culture embodying openness and participation, much of their routine behaviour appeared to be geared towards maintaining and extending their prerogative. The tension between workers' autonomy and the continuing 'business need' for direct management intervention was difficult to resolve in practice, and inhibited the development of workers' commitment. The cultivation of 'open management' did not prove easy in the large workplaces that formed the basis of this study. Under conflicting pressures, the sophistication of the new unitarist ideal did not penetrate very deeply into the British management psyche. The complexity of organisational life prevented managers from fully endorsing all aspects of the 'sophisticated unitarism', revealing that beneath their commitment to a new approach there is a continuing and rather more straightforward desire for enhanced control over work. Their interpretation of the 'new industrial relations' did not lead them to develop successful means of incorporating workers' views in the management of organisations.

It is likely that successful change in industrial relations cannot be achieved quickly. Although the ways in which workplaces adjust to new circumstances may be culturally specific, the evidence presented here suggests that their reform processes are of a conservative nature. Organisational development is likely to be an incremental affair rather than a sudden transformation. But underlying this point is the distinct possibility that even the most sophisticated types of unitarism cannot generate and sustain workers' commitment to corporate goals. Whilst the 'new industrial relations' might succeed to a greater or lesser degree in particular instances, one wonders whether it is possible that unitarism might ever provide the basis of a successful model or paradigm for managing labour relations. Many business decisions inevitably involve difficult choices which will affect various members of an organisation in different ways. Without some means of establishing the widest possible consensus on decisions, one must doubt how far it is possible to build organisations which can respond speedily to the market, whilst maintaining the commitment of employees.

Improving industrial relations will depend not upon obscuring differences of interest between management and workers, but upon improving trust between them. The pluralist approach to managing industrial relations has been much maligned. Its strength, however, was the importance it placed upon providing workers with opportunities to express and resolve their grievances successfully. The evidence presented in this book suggests that where management devoted attention to making this approach work, it yielded substantial flexibility. Management commitment to a joint approach did produce a considerable measure of co-operation. And it is perhaps revealing that 'new industrial relations' policies were adopted by management either where management refused to accept the pluralist approach, or where it was not sufficiently committed to making it work. If, in future, managers reject pluralism in favour of attempts to build a more unitarist culture, the outcome will be uncertain.

The studies presented in the preceding chapters illustrate an essentially simple but important point. A genuine consensus about the goals of an organisation cannot be created by denying that there are differences of interest between workers and managers. Workers' morale and willingness to co-operate with management depends not only upon their being kept well informed of management decisions, but also upon their being able to analyse, challenge, and influence those decisions, without fear of being seen as disloyal or disruptive by management. In both union and non-union workplaces alike, managements should think again about their present interpretation of the 'new industrial relations', and in particular about their approach to employee involvement. Employers must commit themselves to working jointly with employees over as wide a range of issues as possible, by using new joint decision-making techniques. The debate about an organisation's goals and values can often be articulated most clearly through formal channels. In both union and non-union firms, managements should consider developing or extending forms of representative worker participation in decision-making. It is wrong to believe that representative bodies must result inevitably in heated adversarialism. When properly organised, such bodies can provide legitimacy for business decisions which cannot exist when decisions are made by management alone.

If, however, employers maintain their open preference for unitarism, then one is led inescapably towards less sanguine conclusions. No doubt workers' expressions of discontent will continue to be muted, often unspoken, and in the end perhaps even forgotten or set aside. Such circumstances will, however, be unlikely to promote the development of more productive shop floor relations. Unless managers take a broader view of their relations with employees, the search for a committed and co-operative workforce will bring little reward. What is certain is that organisations are likely to experience continuous competitive pressure in the future. British managers may have taken on new ideas, but they have not yet found ways to make them work well on the shop floor. Clearly much remains to be done. Generating commitment will require something broader than unitarism. It will require management to take clear decisions about future industrial relations, make a commitment to more genuine open management, and be prepared to endure additional costs and setbacks in the medium term. The alternative can only be low trust and wasted talent.

Bibliography

ACAS (1987) *Annual Report*, London, ACAS.

(1988a) 'Flexibility in Britain', *Occasional Paper* 41, London, ACAS.

(1988b) *Annual Report*, London, ACAS.

(1989) *Annual Report*, London, ACAS.

(1990) *Annual Report*, London, ACAS.

(1991a) 'Consultation and Communication', *Occasional Paper* 49, London, ACAS.

(1991b) *Annual Report*, London, ACAS.

Ahlstrand, B. (1990) *The Quest for Productivity: the Fawley Productivity Agreements*, Cambridge, Cambridge University Press.

Armstrong, P.J., Goodman, J.F.B. and Hyman, J.D. (1981) *Ideology and Shop Floor Industrial Relations*, London, Croom Helm.

Arthurs, A. (1985a) 'Towards Single Status', *Journal of General Management* 1: 16–28.

(1985b) 'Egalitarianism in the Workplace', in Hammond, V. (ed.), *Current Research in Management*, London, Francis Pinter.

Arthurs, A. and Kinnie, N. (1984) 'Time Up for Clocking?', *Employee Relations* 6(3): 22–5.

Baldamus, W. (1957) 'The Relationship between Wage and Effort', *Journal of Industrial Economics*, 5 July: 192–201.

(1961) *Efficiency and Effort*, Tavistock, London.

Basset, P. (1986) *Strike Free: New Industrial Relations in Britain*, London, Macmillan.

(1987) 'Consultation and the Right to Manage 1980–84', *British Journal of Industrial Relations* 25(2): 283–6.

Batstone, E. (1984) *Working Order*, Oxford, Blackwell.

(1988) *The Reform of Workplace Industrial Relations: Theory, Myth and Evidence*, Oxford, Clarendon.

Batstone, E. Boraston, I. and Frenkel, S. (1977) *Shop Stewards in Action*, Oxford, Blackwell.

Batstone, E., Gourlay S., Levie H. and Moore, R. (1987) *Unions, Unemployment and Innovation*, Oxford, Blackwell.

Behrend, H. (1959) 'Financial Incentives as the Expression of a System of Beliefs', *British Journal of Sociology* 10(2).

159

Belanger, J. (1985) *Job Control and the Institutionalisation of Labour Relations in the Workplace: A Study of Two Engineering Firms in England*, Ph.D thesis, University of Warwick.

(1987) 'Job Control After Reform: a Case Study of Engineering', *Industrial Relations Journal* 17(2): 50–62.

Belanger, J. and Evans, S. (1988) 'Job Controls and Shop Steward Leadership Among Semi-skilled Engineering Workers', in Terry, M. and Edwards, P.K. (eds.), *Shop Floor Politics and Job Controls: the Post-war Engineering Industry*, Oxford, Blackwell.

Bennet, A. and Smith-Gavine, S. (1988) 'The Percentage Utilisation of Labour Index (PUL)', in Bosworth, D. (ed.), *Working Below Capacity*, London, Macmillan.

Berg, I., Freedman, M. and Freeman, M. (1978) *Managers and Work Reform: a Limited Engagement, New York*, Free Press.

Beynon, H. (1985) *Working for Ford* (2nd edition), London, Pelican.

Blackler, F. and Brown C. (1980) *Whatever Happened to Shell's New Philosophy of Management?*, Farnborough, Saxon House.

Boulter, N. (1982) 'Breaking the Mould of BL's Industrial Relations', *Personnel Management*, September: 20–4.

Bradley, K. and Hill, S. (1983) 'After Japan: the Quality Circle Transplant and Productive Efficiency', *British Journal of Industrial Relations* 21(3): 292–311.

Brook, L., Hedges, S., Jowell, R., Lewis, J., Prior, G., Sebastian, G., Taylor, B. and Witherspoon, S. (1992) *British Social Attitudes Cumulative Sourcebook: the First Six Surveys*, Aldershot, Gower.

Brown, W. (1972) 'A Consideration of Custom and Practice', *British Journal of Industrial Relations* 10: 32–61.

(1973) *Piecework Bargaining*, London, Heineman.

(1981) *The Changing Contours of British Industrial Relations*, Oxford, Blackwell.

(1983) 'Britain's Unions: New Pressures and Shifting Loyalties', *Personnel Management*, October: 48–50.

(1986) 'The Changing Role of Trade Unions in the Management of Labour', *British Journal of Industrial Relations* 24(2).

Brown, W. and Sisson, K. (1975) 'The Use of Comparisons in Workplace Wage Determination', *British Journal of Industrial Relations* 13: 23–53.

Brown W. and Wadhwani, S. (1990) 'The Economic Effects of Industrial Relations Legislation Since 1979', *National Institute Economic Review* 131: 57–70.

Buchanan, D. (1987) 'Job Enrichment is Dead: Long Live High Performance Work Design!', *Personnel Management*, May: 40–3.

Buchanan, D. and McCalman, J. (1989) *High Performance Work Systems: the Digital Experience*, London, Routledge.

Bullock (1977) Royal Commission of Inquiry on Industrial Democracy, *Report*, Cmnd 6706, London, HMSO.

Burawoy, M. (1979) *Manufacturing Consent: Changes in the Labour Process under Monopoly Capitalism*, Chicago, Chicago University Press.

Burns, T. and Stalker, G.M. (1961) *The Management of Innovation*, London, Tavistock.

Cadbury, Sir Adrian (1985) 'The 1980s: A Watershed in British Industrial Relations?', the fourth Hitachi lecture, delivered at the University of Sussex,

Institute of Manpower Studies, Unit for Comparative Research on Industrial Relations.

Capelli, P. and McKersie, R. (1987) 'Management Strategy and the Redesign of Workrules', *Journal of Management Studies* 24(5): 441–62.

Cavendish, R. (1982) *Women on the Line*, London, Routledge & Kegan Paul.

Chadwick, M.G. (1983) 'The Recession and Industrial Relations: a Factory Approach', *Employee Relations* 5(5): 5–12.

Clegg, H. (1979) *The Changing System of Industrial Relations in Great Britain*, Oxford, Blackwell.

Confederation of British Industry (1981) *The Will to Win*, London, CBI.

Cressey, P., Eldridge, J. and MacInnes, J. (1985) *Just Managing: Authority and Democracy in Industry*, Buckingham, Open University Press.

Cunninson, S. (1966) *Wages and Work Allocation: a Study of Social Relations in a Garment Workshop*, London, Tavistock.

Daniel, W. and Millward N. (1983) *Workplace Industrial Relations in Britain: The DE/PSI/ESRC Survey*, London, Heinemann.

Dawson, P. and Webb, J. (1989) 'New Production Arrangements: the Totally Flexible Cage?', *Work Employment and Society* 3(2): 231–8.

Deming, W. (1970) *Statistical Control of Quality in Japan*, Tokyo, Union of Japanese Scientists and Engineers.

Dickson, T., McLachan, H.V., Prior, P. and Swales, K. (1988) 'Big Blue and the Unions: IBM, Individualism and Trade Union Strategy', *Work Employment and Society* 2(4): 506–20.

Donovan (1968) Royal Commission on Trade Unions and Employers Associations, *Report*, Cmnd 3623, London, HMSO.

Edwards, P.K. (1985a) 'Managing Labour Relations through the Recession', *Employee Relations* 7(2): 3–7.

(1985b) 'Managing Through the Recession: the Plant and the Company', *Employee Relations* 3(2): 4–8.

(1986) *Conflict at Work*, Oxford, Blackwell.

(1987) *Managing the Factory*, Oxford, Blackwell.

(1988) 'Patterns of Conflict and Accommodation', in Gallie, D. (ed.), *Employment in Britain* Oxford, Blackwell: 187–217.

(1989) 'Three Faces of Discipline', in Sisson, K. (ed.), *Personnel Management in Britain* Oxford, Blackwell, 296–325.

Edwards, P.K. and Scullion, H. (1982) *The Social Organisation of Workplace Conflict*, Oxford, Blackwell.

(1991a) 'Industrial Conflict: a Review of the Research', paper prepared for the British Universities Industrial Relations Association Conference, Manchester.

(1991b) 'The Political Economy of Conflict and the Ethnographic Tradition of Workplace Studies: Themes and Issues in Comparative Research', paper prepared for Conference on 'Workplace Industrial Relations and Industrial Conflict in Comparative Perspective', University of Laval, Quebec, Canada.

(1992) 'Comparative Industrial Relations: The Contribution of the Ethnographic Tradition', *Relations Industrielles*.

Edwards, P.K. and Whitson, C. (1989a) 'The Control of Absenteeism: an Interim Report', *Warwick Papers in Industrial Relations*, 23, Coventry, University of Warwick Industrial Relations Research Unit.

(1989b) 'Industrial Discipline, the Control of Attendance and the Subordination of Labour: Towards an Integrated Analysis', *Work, Employment and Society* 3(1): 1–28.

Edwards, R. (1979) *Contested Terrain: the Transformation of the Workplace in the Twentieth Century*, London, Heineman.

Elger, T. (1989) 'Flexible Futures?: New Technology and the Contemporary Transformation of Work', *Work, Employment and Society* 1(4): 528–40.

Employment Protection Act 1975, Chapter 71, London, HMSO.

Evansohn, J. (1989) 'The Effects of Mechanisms of Managerial Control on Unionization', *Industrial Relations*, 28(1): 91–103.

Findlay, P. (1992) 'Union Recognition and Non-Unionism: Shifting Fortunes in the Electronics Industry in Scotland' *Industrial Relations Journal* 23(4).

Foulkes, F. (1980) *Personnel Policies in Large Non-union Companies*, Englewood Cliffs, N.J., Prentice Hall.

Fox, A. (1974) *Beyond Contract: Work, Power and Trust Relations*, London, Faber & Faber.

(1985) *Man Mismanagement* (2nd edition), London, Hutchinson.

Fox, A. and Flanders, A. (1975) 'The Reform of Collective Bargaining: from Donovan to Durkheim', in Flanders, A., *Management and Unions*: London, Faber & Faber, 241–76.

Friedman, A. (1977) *Industry and Labour: Class Struggle at Work and Monopoly Capitalism*, London, Macmillan.

Gallie, D. (1978) *In Search of the New Working Class*, Cambridge, Cambridge University Press.

(1983) *Social Inequality and Class Radicalism in France and Britain*, Cambridge, Cambridge University Press.

Garrahan, P. and Stewart, P. (1989) 'Post-Fordism, Japanisation and the Local Economy', paper given to Conference of Socialist Economists, Sheffield, July.

Geary, J.F. (1992a) 'Employment Flexibility and Human Resource Management: The Case of Three American Electronics Plants', *Work, Employment and Society* 6(2): 251–70.

(1992b) 'Pay, Control and Commitment', *Human Resource Management Journal* 2(4): 36–54.

Glaser, B.G. and Strauss, A.L. (1968) *The Discovery of Grounded Theory*, London, Aldine Press.

Gouldner, A. (1955) *Wildcat Strike*, London, Routledge & Kegan Paul.

Gregson, D. and Ruffle, K. (1980) 'Rationalising Rewards at Rogerstone', *Personnel Management* October: 62–4.

Griffen, R.W. (1988) 'Consequences of Quality Circles in an Industrial Setting: a Longitudinal Assessment', *Academy Management Journal* 31(2): 338–58.

Guest, D. (1989a) 'Human Resource Management: its Implications for Industrial Relations and Trade Unions', in Storey, J. (ed.), *New Perspectives on Human Resource Management*: 41–55.

(1989b) 'Personnel and HRM: Can You Tell the Difference?' *Personnel Management*, January: 48–52.

(1990) 'Have British Workers been Working Harder in Thatcher's Britain?: a Reconsideration of the Concept of Effort', *British Journal of Industrial Relations* 28(3): 293–312.

(1991) 'Personnel Management: the End of Orthodoxy?', *British Journal of Industrial Relations*: 149–75.

Hammersley, M. (1990) *Reading Ethnographic Research, A Critical Guide*, Harlow, Longman.

Harris, R. (1987) *Power and Powerlessness in Industry*, London, Tavistock.

Hendry, C. and Pettigrew, A. (1986) 'The Practice of Strategic Human Resource Management', *Personnel Review* 15(5): 3–8.

Hendry, C., Pettigrew, A. and Sparrow, P. (1988) 'Changing Patterns of Human Resource Management', *Personnel Management*, November: 37–41.

Hyman, R. (1970) 'Economic Motivation and Labour Stability', *British Journal of Industrial Relations* 8(2): 159–78.

Incomes Data Services (1986a) *Flexibility at Work*, IDS Study 360.

(1986b) *Flexible Working Practices: Trick or Treat?*, IDS Report 464.

Industrial Relations Services, 'Komatsu: the first year of a new start', *Review and Report* 391 2–6.

'Harmonisation: 2 – pressures for change', *Review and Report* 452: 13–14

Ingram, P.N. (1991) 'Changes in Working Practices in British Manufacturing Industry in the 1980s: A Study of Employee Concessions Made During Wage Negotiations', *British Journal of Industrial Relations* 29(1): 1–13.

Jackson, P. (1983) 'How Perkins Positively Tackled the Recession', *Personnel Management* November: 24–7.

Juran, J.N. (1976) *Quality Control Handbook*, New York, McGraw Hill.

Katz, H.C., Kochan, T.A. and Weber, M.R. (1985) 'Assessing the Effects of Industrial Relations Systems and Efforts to Improve the Quality of Working Life and Organizational Effectiveness', *Academy of Management Journal* 28(3): 509–26.

Katz, H.C., Thomas, A., Kochan, A. and Gobielle, K.R. (1983) 'Industrial Relations Performance, Economic Performance, and QWL Programs: an Interplant Analysis', *Industrial and Labor Relations Review*, 37(1): 3–17.

Kelly, J. (1982) *Scientific Management, Job Redesign and Work Performance*, London, Academic Press.

(1987) 'Trade Unions Through the Recession 1980–84', *British Journal of Industrial Relations* 25(2): 275–82.

Kelly, J. and Kelly, C. (1991) '"Them and Us": Social Psychology and the New Industrial Relations', *British Journal of Industrial Relations* 29(1): 25–48.

Kelly, J. and Richardson, R. (1989) 'Annual Review 1988', *British Journal of Industrial Relations* 27(2): 133–54.

Kemp N., Clegg C. and Wall T. (1980) 'Job Redesign: Content Process and Outcomes', *Employee Relations* 2(5): 5–14.

Kennedy, G. (1988) 'Single Status as the Key to Flexibility', *Personnel Management*, February: 51–3.

Klein, J.A. (1984) 'Why do Supervisors Resist Employee Involvement?', *Harvard Business Review*, September/October: 87–95.

Kochan, T.A. and Dyer, L. (1976) 'A Model of Organisational Change in the Context of Union Management Relations', *The Journal of Applied Behavioural Science* 12: 59–78.

Kochan, T.A., Katz, H.C. and McKersie, R.B. (1986) *The Transformation of American Industrial Relations*, New York, Basic Books.

Lawler, E.E. and Mohrman, S.A. (1987) 'Quality circles: After the Honeymoon', *Organizational Dynamics* 15(4): 42–54.

Legge, K. (1988) 'Personnel Management in Recession and Recovery: a Comparative Analysis of What the Surveys Say', *Personnel Review* 17(2).

— (1989) 'Human Resource Management: a Critical Analysis', in Storey, J. (ed.), *New Perspectives on Human Resource Management*, London, Routledge.

Lever-Tracey, C. (1990) 'The Supervisor and the Militant Shop Steward: Evidence from the Australian Motor Industry', *Journal of Industrial Relations* 27(3): 335–49.

Lewis, P. (1989) 'Employee Participation in a Japanese Owned British Electronics Factory: Reality or Symbolism', *Employee Relations* 11(1): 3–9.

Lincoln, J.R. and Kalleberg, A.L. (1990) *Culture, Control and Commitment*, Cambridge, Cambridge University Press.

Lupton, T. (1961) 'Money for Effort', *Problems of Progress in Industry* 11, Ministry of Technology, London, HMSO.

— (1963) *On the Shop Floor*, Oxford, Pergamon Press.

MacInnes, J. (1986) 'Conjuring Up Consultation: the Role and Extent of Joint Consultation in Post-war Private Manufacturing Industry', *British Journal of Industrial Relations* 24: 93–113.

— (1988) *Thatcherism at Work*, Buckingham, Open University Press.

Mackay, L. (1986) 'The Macho-Manager: It's no Myth', *Personnel Management*, January: 25–7.

Marchington, M. (1990) 'Analysing the Link between Product Markets and the Management of Industrial Relations', *Journal of Management Studies* 27(2): 111–32.

Marchington, M. and Parker, P. (1988) 'Japanization: a Lack of Chemical Reaction', *Industrial Relations Journal* 19(4): 272–85.

— (1990) *Changing Patterns of Employee Relations*, Hemel Hempstead, Harvester Wheatsheaf.

Marchington, M., Goodman, J., Wilkinson, A., Ackers, P. (1992) *New Developments in Employee Involvement*, Research Series 2, London, Employment Department.

Marsden, D. (1985) *The Car Industry: Labour Relations and Industrial Adjustment*, London, Tavistock.

Marsden, D. and Thompson, M. (1990) 'Flexibility Agreements and their Significance in The Increase in Productivity in British Manufacturing since 1980', *Work, Employment and Society* 4(1): 83–104.

McCarthy, W.E.J. and Ellis, N. (1973) *Management by Agreement: an alternative to the Industrial Relations Act*, London, Hutchinson.

McKersie, R.B. (1987) 'The Transformation of American Industrial Relations: the Abridged Story', *Journal of Management Studies* 24(5): 433–40.

McLaughlin, I. and Beardwell, I. (1989) *Non-unionism and the Non-union Firm in British Industrial Relations*, Kingston, Kingston Business School.

Metcalf, D. (1989a) 'Can Unions Survive in the Private Sector?', Working Paper 1130, London, London School of Economics.

— (1989b) 'Water Notes Dry Up: the Impact of the Donovan Reform Proposals and Thatcherism at Work on Labour Productivity in British Manufacturing Industry', *British Journal of Industrial Relations* 27(1): 1–31.

Millward, N. (1972) 'Piecework Earnings and Workers' Controls', *Human Relations*, 25 September: 351–76.

Millward, N. and Stevens, M. (1986) *British Workplace Industrial Relations 1980–84: The DE/ESRC/PSI/ACAS Survey*, Aldershot, Gower.

Millward, N., Stevens, M., Smart, D. and Hawes, W. (1992) *Workplace Industrial Relations in Transition: The DE/ESRC/PSI/ACAS Survey*, Aldershot, Dartmouth.

Mitchell, J.C. (1983) 'Case and Situation Analysis', *Sociological Review*: 187–211.

Morris, T. and Wood, S. (1991) 'Testing the Survey Method: Continuity and Change in British Industrial Relations', *Work, Employment and Society* 5(2): 259–82.

Mullins, T. (1986) 'Harmonisation: the Benefits and the Lessons', *Personnel Management*, March: 38–41.

Nichols, T. and Beynon, H. (1977) *Living with Capitalism: Class Relations in the Modern Factory*, London, Routledge & Kegan Paul.

Nichols, T. (1986) *The British Worker Question: a New Look at Workers and Productivity in Manufacturing*, London, Routledge and Kegan Paul.

(1990) 'Industrial Relations and British Manufacturing', *Bulletin of Comparative Labour Relations* 20: 39–61.

Nolan, P. (1988) 'Pay, Productivity and U.K. Industrial Performance: An Overview', position paper for Warwick /IRS Conference, 'Pay, Performance and Productivity', 9–10 February, University of Warwick, Coventry.

Nolan, P. and Brown, W. (1988) 'Wages and Labour Productivity: The Contribution of Industrial Relations Research to the Understanding of Pay Determination', *British Journal of Industrial Relations* 26(3): 339–62.

Oliver, N. and Davies, A. (1990) 'Adopting Japanese Style Manufacturing Methods: a Tale of Two (U.K.) Factories', *Journal of Management Studies* 27(5): 555–70.

Oliver, N. and Wilkinson, B. (1988) *The Japanisation of British Industry*, Oxford, Blackwell.

(1989a) 'Japanese Manufacturing Techniques and Personnel and Industrial Relations Practice in Britain: Evidence and Issues', *British Journal of Industrial Relations* 27(1): 73–91.

(1989b) 'Power, Control and the Kanban', *Journal of Management Studies* 26(1): 47–58.

Parker, S. (1975) *Workplace Industrial Relations, 1972*, London, HMSO.

Peach, L.H. (1983) 'Employee Relations at IBM', *Employee Relations* 5(3): 17–20.

Pegge, T. (1986) 'Hitachi Two Years On', *Personnel Management*, October: 42–7.

Peters, T. and Waterman, R. (1982) *In Search of Excellence*, New York, Harper and Row.

Phelps-Brown, H. (1949) 'Morale, Military and Industrial', *The Economic Journal*, March: 40–55.

(1990) 'The Counter-revolution of our Time', *Industrial Relations* 29(1): 1–15.

Pollert, A. (1981) *Girls, Wives, Factory Lives*, London, Macmillan.

Price, R. (1989) 'The Decline of the Status Divide', in Sisson, K. (ed.), *Personnel Management in Britain*, Oxford, Blackwell: 271–92.

Purcell, J. (1979) 'The Lessons of the Commission on Industrial Relations', *Industrial Relations Journal* 14(2): 4–22.

(1981) *Good Industrial Relations*, London, Macmillan.
(1982) 'Macho Managers and the New Industrial Relations', *Employee Relations* 4(1): 3–5.
(1983) 'Management Control through Collective Bargaining: a Future Strategy', in Thurley, K. and Wood, S. (eds.), *Industrial relations and management strategy*, Cambridge, Cambridge University Press.
(1987) 'Mapping out Management Styles', *Journal of Management Studies* 24(5): 533–48.
Purcell, J. and Sisson, K. (1983) 'Strategies and Practice in the Management of Industrial Relations', in Bain, G.S (ed.), *Industrial relations in Britain*, Oxford, Blackwell: 95–120.
Richardson, R. and Wood, S. (1989) 'Productivity in the Coal Industry and the New Industrial Relations', *British Journal of Industrial Relations* 27(1), March.
Rogers, W. and Hammersley, J.M. (1954), 'The Consistency of Stop Watch Time Study Practitioners', *Occupational Psychology* 28(2).
Rose, M. (1988) 'Attachment to Work and Social Values', in Gallie, D. (ed.) *Employment in Britain*, Oxford, Blackwell: 128–56.
Rose, H., McLoughlin, I., King, R. and Clark, J. (1986) 'Opening the Black Box: the Relation Between Technology and Work', *New Technology, Work and Employment* 1(1): 18–26.
Roy, D. (1952) 'Efficiency and "the Fix": Informal Inter-group Relations in a Piecework Machine Shop', *American Journal of Sociology*, 57: 255–66.
(1955) 'Quota Restriction and Goldbricking in a Machine Shop', *American Journal of Sociology* 60: 427–42.
Roy, D. (1970) 'The Study of Southern Labor Union Organising Campaigns', in Habenstein, R. (ed.), *Pathways to Data*, 216–44, Chicago, Aldine Press.
Sayles, L. (1958) *The Behaviour of Industrial Workgroups: Prediction and Control*, New York, John Wiley.
Scott, A. (1991) 'Consultation and Communication: the 1990 ACAS Survey', *Employment Gazette*, September.
Sewell, G. and Wilkinson, B. (1992) '"Someone to watch over me": Surveillance, Discipline, and the Just-in-Time Labour Process', *Sociology*, 26(2), May 271–89.
Sisson, K. (1984) 'Changing Strategies in Industrial Relations', *Personnel Management*, May: 24–7.
Smith, C., Child, J. and Rowlinson, M. (1991) *Reshaping Work: the Cadbury Experience*, Cambridge, Cambridge University Press.
Smith, D. (1988) 'The Japanese Example in South West Birmingham', *Industrial Relations Journal* 19(1): 41–50.
Spencer, B. (1985) 'Shop Steward Resistance in the Recession', *Employee Relations* 7(5): 22–8.
Stevens, M. and Wareing, A. (1990), 'Union Density and Workforce Composition: Preliminary Results from the 1989 Labour Force Survey', *Employment Gazette*, August: 403–11.
Storey, J. (1988) 'The People Management Dimension in Current Programmes of Organisational Change' *Employee Relations* 10(6): 17–25.
(1989) 'Introduction: From Personnel Management to Human Resource Management', in Storey, J. (ed.), *New Perspectives on Human Resource Management*, London, Routledge.

(1992) 'HRM in Action: the Truth is Out at Last', *Personnel Management* April: 28–31.

Storey, J. and Sisson, K. (1990) 'Limits to Transformation: Human Resource Management in the British Context', *Industrial Relations Journal* 21(1): 60–5.

Tailby, S. and Whitson, C. (eds.) (1989) 'Industrial Relations and Restructuring' in *Manufacturing Change: Industrial Relations and Restructuring*, Oxford, Blackwell.

Terry, M. (1978) 'The Inevitable Growth of Informality', *British Journal of Industrial Relations* 15(1): 76–90.

(1979) 'Shop Stewards: the Emergence of a Lay Elite?', Industrial Relations Research Unit Discussion Paper 14, University of Warwick, Coventry.

(1983a) 'Shop Steward Development and Managerial Strategies', in Bain, G.S. (ed.), *Industrial Relations in Britain*, Oxford, Blackwell: 69–74.

(1983b) 'Shop Stewards Through Expansion and Recession', *Industrial Relations Journal* 14(3): 49–58.

(1986) 'How Do We Know If Shop Stewards are Getting Weaker?', *British Journal of Industrial Relations* 24(2): 169–79.

(1988) *Toshiba's New British Company: Competitiveness Through Innovation in Industry*, London, Policy Studies Institute.

(1989) 'Recontextualising Shop Floor Industrial Relations: Some Case Study Evidence', in Tailby, S. and Whitson, C. (eds.), *Manufacturing Change: Industrial Relations and Restructuring*, Oxford, Blackwell.

Thurley, K. and Wood, S. (eds.) (1983) *Industrial Relations and Management Strategy*, Cambridge, Cambridge University Press.

Trevor, M. and White, M. (1983) *Under Japanese Management*, London, Heinemann.

Wall, T., Kemp, N., Jackson, P. and Clegg C. (1986) 'Outcomes of Autonomous Workgroups: a Long Term Field Experiment', *Academy of Management Journal* 29(2): 280–304.

Walton, R. (1985) 'From Control to Commitment in the Workplace', *Harvard Business Review*, March/April: 76–84.

Walton, R. and McKersie, R.A. (1965) *A Behavioural Theory of Labour Negotiations: an Analysis of a Social Interaction System*, New York, McGraw-Hill.

Wells, D.M (1987) *Empty Promises: Quality of Working Life Programs and the Labor Movement*, New York, Monthly Review Press.

Westwood, S. (1983) *All Day Every Day: Factory and Family in the Making of Womens' Lives*, London, Pluto.

White, M. and Trevor, M. (1983) *Under Japanese Management: the Experience of British Workers*, London, Policy Studies Institute.

Wickens, P. (1985) 'Nissan: the Thinking Behind the Union Agreement', *Personnel Management*, August: 18–21.

(1987) *The Road to Nissan: Flexibility, Quality, Teamwork*, London, Macmillan.

(1988) 'Management in the fast track: Can the Unions Adapt?', the seventh Hitachi lecture, delivered at the University of Sussex, Institute of Manpower Studies, Unit for Comparative Research on Industrial Relations, *Institute of Manpower Studies Report* 159.

Wilkinson, A., Allen, P. and Snape, E. (1991) 'TQM and the Management of Labour', *Employee Relations* 13(1): 24–31.

Wilkinson, B. (1983) *The Shop Floor Politics of New Technology*, London, Heineman.
Williams, K. (1983) 'Introduction', in Williams, K., Williams, D. and Thomas, D. (eds.) *Why are the British So Bad at Manufacturing?*, London, Routledge & Kegan Paul.
Williams, K., Williams, J. and Haslam, C. (1989) 'Do Labour Costs Really Matter?', *Work, Employment and Society* 3(2): 281–305.
Willman, P. (1980) 'Leadership and Trade Union Principles: Some Problems of Management Sponsorship and Independence', *Industrial Relations Journal* 11(4): 39–49.
 (1982) *Fairness, Collective Bargaining and Incomes Policy*, Oxford, Clarendon Press.
Willman, P. and Winch, G. (1985) *Innovation and Management Control: labour relations in BL Cars*, Cambridge, Cambridge University Press.

Index

absence, 19, 89
Advisory Conciliation and Arbitration
  Service (ACAS), 1, 27
appraisal, 11, 12, 98
aptitude tests, 119
attitude surveys, 28, 36
Australia, 22
automation, 81, 85, 99
  see also new technology
autonomous work groups, 19, 41, 44, 47–8,
  69, 142–3
  failure of, 58, 59
  reactions to, 48–58, 64–5

biscuit works
  and ban on unofficial overtime, 88
  and control of unions, 76–7, 93
  'culture of politeness' in, 86–91, 93, 94,
    154
  discipline in, 79–80, 87, 88
  fieldwork for, 34, 39
  and influence of past practices, 150
  joint approach, 71–2, 73, 75, 79–82,
    128–9
  low wages in, 86
  management policy a qualified success,
    94–5
  management–union relations in, 34, 147
  and managers' resistance to unions, 74
  production process, 77–8
  reorganisation of production, 72, 73
  role of managers in, 78–9, 81–2
  success of pay policy, 139
  and tightening of discipline, 89–90
  and union recognition, 33, 40, 72–3, 75,
    91–3
  weakness of unions in, 85
  workers' attitudes to unions, 92–3
  and workers' reactions to job losses, 85
  workers' views on unemployment and
    job security, 134–6
bonus schemes, 99, 103, 121, 139

British Social Attitudes Surveys, 18
'bulk box' dispute, 62, 67

capital investments, 31
case-studies, 28–40
  evidence in, 35–40
  fieldwork for, 33–5
  generalising from, 29–31
  value of, 30
change *see* management change
chocolate works, 33, 40
  changes in production process, 106–8
  and changes in management–worker
    relations, 144, 145–6, 148
  company philosophy of, 97–8, 122–3,
    129
  and 'Company Principles', 101–2, 105,
    112, 113, 114, 118, 122
  and conflicts over discipline, 112–15, 143
  consultation procedures, 115–17
  contradictions in management policy,
    130
  disputes between workers, 110–11
  egalitarian approach to rewards, 102–3
  failure of communication in, 118, 124
  fieldwork for, 34, 39
  and influence of past, 150, 151
  lack of commitment, 123–4, 154
  management control in, 105–6, 110–12,
    128
  new approach to labour relations, 100–1
  payments system, 118–22, 138
  reorganisation of work, 103–4, 140, 141,
    142
  sought climate of agreement, 105
  and tensions between workers and
    managers, 113–14
  and 'wage–effort bargain', 99, 133
  workers' views on unemployment and
    job security, 134–6
clocking on, 47, 54, 89, 99
cold store workers, 62

169

Cambridge Studies in Management

Printed in the United States
By Bookmasters